Illustrated
Morgan
BUYER'S GUIDE ™

Three-wheelers and four-wheelers model-by-model analysis from 1909

Ken Hill

Motorbooks International
Publishers & Wholesalers Inc.
Osceola, Wisconsin 54020, USA

First published in 1989 by Motorbooks
International Publishers & Wholesalers Inc, P O
Box 2, 729 Prospect Avenue, Osceola, WI 54020
USA

Printed and bound in the United States of
America

Library of Congress Cataloging-in-Publication Data

Hill, Ken
 Illustrated Morgan buyer's guide.

 1. Morgan automobile—Purchasing. I. Title.
TL215.M57H545 1989   629.2'222   88-13731
ISBN 0-87938-214-7 (soft)

On the front cover: An early Morgan Plus 8.
John H. Sheally II

On the back cover: A 1928 Super Sports Aero.
John H. Sheally II

Contents

Acknowledgments

No book of this type can be written without the unstinting cooperation of many people, all of whom are experts in their own fields. Without their help, this book would never have reached the publisher.

First, I record my thanks to Peter Morgan and Charles Morgan and the staff of the Morgan Motor Company for unfailing assistance once again, with the provision of production records, photographs and material from their archives.

I am also indebted to Michael Ware and Linda Springate of the National Motor Museum for placing their expertise, library and records at my disposal; to Sarah Joselin LBIPP, LMPA, and Dave Miller LIIP, AMPA, for all their expert photographic advice and assistance and also for the loan of special photographic equipment.

With respect to the three-wheeler section of this book, I would like to extend my sincere thanks to Nev' Lear for proofreading and to Chris Booth, Brian Watts and Larry Ayres for all their advice and technical information. Also a special thank you to Derek Rushton for supplying so many of the previously unpublished photographs and, of course, for his advice.

My belated, but nevertheless sincere, thanks to John H. Sheally II, who has supplied me with an abundance of photographs over the years, many of which are used in this book.

Next, I must thank Barry Iles, general secretary of the Morgan Sports Car Club, who saved me hours of research by supplying an up-to-date list of Morgan club contacts around the world.

I have obtained information from material and notes left by the late Dick Pritchard. He had collected material for over forty years or more, and the exact origin of much of it is unknown. I know that he assembled material from most motoring magazines, including *Light Car & Cycle Car; Motor Cycle; Motor Cycling; Autosport; Motor Sport; Motor; and Autocar*. In addition, I have collected material over the past twenty years from magazines, Morgan clubs and Morgan owners from all over the world. In many cases, it is now impossible to establish the exact source of certain material, photographs and information, and therefore I sincerely thank all these writers, photographers, magazines and others who have helped me with some of the detail of this book.

Finally, as always I express my thanks to my wife, Janet, who once again has helped me so much in the research and compiling of a book.

Ken Hill

Introduction

*"I can reel off
more reasons for
not buying a
Morgan than for
buying one."*

Peter Morgan
Managing Director
Morgan Motor Company Limited
in a press interview, 1988

To visit the Morgan factory at Pickersleigh Road, Malvern Link, Worcestershire, England, which nestles at the foot of the Malvern Hills, is to enter a time warp. You have stepped into the 1920s or 1930s. Admittedly, there are modern telephones, a small table-top photostat machine, an up-to-date, but not automated, paint shop, modern engines in the cars, some other modern equipment and a few other trappings of the 1980s—but there it ends.

Morgans to this day are built in the vintage coachbuilding tradition. For this reason, no two Morgans are ever exactly the same. To drive even the most recent model is to experience a type of motoring that most older people have long since forgotten or that younger people have never been privileged to experience.

If you are looking for such things as soft springing, power-assisted steering and power hoods, then look elsewhere. Do not, under any circumstances, even consider buying a Morgan.

If you want to experience the wind in your hair, with quite possibly some oil thrown in; a drive during which, when you turn the steering wheel, the front wheels respond immediately rather than a second later; a hard ride where every small bump, pothole, ridge, white line and matchstick can be felt through your backside; g-forces from an ordinary roadgoing car; and above all, the thrill and exhilaration of your being in charge of a sports car rather than its being in charge of you; plus all those indescribable experiences and feelings, which combine to give you the motoring thrill of a lifetime—then buy a Morgan.

Before you rush off to try to buy the last of the real sports cars, let me at least try to help you by telling you what you should do and look for in your pursuit. First and foremost, join a Morgan club. You will receive regular newsletters or magazines full of useful information. In addition, attend some of their meets, no matter how far you have to travel to get there. Here you will find sympathetic and equally infected addicts, most of whom will be only too willing to help and advise you on how to find the car of your dreams. You may even find one or two who are attempting the "cold turkey" treatment, having been forced to sell their beloved cars, for one reason or other. You will find a list of

clubs and addresses at the rear of this book. There is no one club for Morgans, either nationally or internationally, which is all in keeping with the individuality and originality of Morgans.

Before buying

Inspect as many examples of the marque as possible before making up your mind which model you most desire. Learn all you can about the Morgan marque, by reading this and some of the other books that have been published. The more you learn, the better equipped you are to make a sound purchase.

Yet again, a word of warning! What you may desire and what you can afford are usually vastly different things. Do not be carried away by enthusiasm. Remember it is not always a good policy to buy a basket case, as the cost of restoration can be enormous and may well be out of all proportion to the value

Every Morgan enthusiast's dream: an original and complete Morgan in need of restoration. This Family three-wheeler was discovered by chance in the United States and has now been restored to 100 point condition. *John H. Sheally II*

of the finished product. It could well be less expensive in the long term to buy a younger model in good condition, and then you not only save money, but you also get to use your new purchase immediately. Should you be lucky enough to find one of the rarer models like a drophead coupe, a Plus 4 Plus, a Plus 4 Super Sports or even a Le Mans Special, then go for it! The cost of restoration will be well invested because the value of these models continues to rise.

All club magazines have a sales advertisement page, and you may find the car of your dreams there. Remember, however, these are enthusiasts' cars, and as such, they could be overvalued. Yet as with most enthusiast-owned items, they could well be in top condition. Other advertisements for Morgans are to be found in motoring publications.

In the 1950s and 1960s, Morgans were imported into the United States by Fergus Motors in New York and by Cox & Pulver in Los Angeles; it is therefore a good idea to check the classified ads in the *New York Times* and *Los Angeles Times*. So many Morgans were sold in these areas that they are good for finding the recently discovered examples, as well as normal sales.

I sound a word of caution about buying a Morgan from overseas and importing it into the United States. Let's take a good hard look at the idea. First, unless stated otherwise, all cars advertised in the United Kingdom are right-hand drive, and although perfectly legal to drive in the United States, this makes for a hairy ride especially during the overtake. The exception to the right- or left-hand drive decision is solved for you with a three-wheeler; you have no choice, they were only made with right-hand drive. The importation of motor vehicles into the United States is a complicated process and requires much expertise. I suggest that you first contact a US Morgan club to obtain advice. Many print details on the correct way to go about importation appear in their club magazines from time to time. In addition, a few US Morgan specialist firms may well be able to assist.

When you have found the car that could well meet your desires, then if at all possible hire a Morgan expert appraiser or a profes-

Unmistakably a Morgan three-wheeler, but which model? A beautiful example of a bitsa. The filler caps suggest a Sports model; the staggered seats and scuttle plus the height of the exhaust, a Super Sports; and the spare wheel mounting, a Sports—all cleverly done, and in good taste, but still a bitsa.

This clever conversion of the bodywork to create a Morgan pickup was carried out by Steve Miller of San Francisco in the late 1970s. *Roger Moran*

sional mechanic (knowledge of British sports cars would help) to examine the car for you. A few hours work by such an expert will reveal nearly all you need to know about your possible purchase. A word of warning here! Make sure you hire someone who knows what he or she is doing, not a "kicker" as they are known in the trade, the "expert" whose main contribution to the proceedings is to kick each tire in turn. There are far too many of these people about, and they can cost you a lot of money.

If you meet opposition from the seller to such an examination, then walk away and find yourself another used Morgan to look at. Even in the United States, an alternative always appears provided you have the patience to wait. Those sellers who object usually have something to hide. If it is a rare model, then you are on your own; even rare models can have expensive hidden faults.

Should you be lucky enough to find a rare model and should the owner have no objections to the detail examination, then be prepared to have to agree to most of the seller's terms, including the price. Some owners who are forced to sell will not even deal if they do not like your looks or if they consider you are not the right kind of person to own their car. Oh yes, it does happen! Morgan owners can be most peculiar.

When you see your dream for the first time, try to resist rushing up and throwing your arms around it. The detached approach is always the best. Remember, as the purchaser you have the advantage (or should have). Apparent indifference could save you $200 to $300, or even more with luck.

First, stand back from the car and scrutinize it from every angle. Observe if it sits squarely on level ground. Check the ground for signs of oil leaks or other fluid leaks. This general observation should reveal if the car has been crashed or suffered other damage, which the seller may be attempting to cover up.

If possible, take with you a detailed concours judging sheet—not that you are looking for a 100 point example, but because this sheet lists every major section of the car. Use it as a checklist for finding things that can be classed as requiring work and therefore could be used when the serious work of negotiating the price begins. Forget minor items—focusing on them only antagonizes the seller and makes negotiations even more difficult.

Buyer beware

Until recent years, Morgans have not been rustproofed or treated with wood preservative. Therefore, the two main troubles with used Morgans are rust and wood rot.

Let us deal with the rust first. You can find rust nearly anywhere on the car, but some places are more likely than others. First check where the fenders and the running boards fit to the body. Until recently, all Morgans were painted with their fenders on. Therefore, the seams had only an undercoat and piping between them. They were then painted over the whole joint, and this completed the water seal. Morgans have a flexible chassis—this in time cracks the paint at the joints, and water seeps in to do untold damage over the years. Other trouble areas to check are the edges of the headlamp nacelles, any other body seams and side moldings on the tail panel. The strips under the doors are the location of a joint in the body panels on some models; in some cases the seam is covered with filler and painted over. This is not original and could indicate the hiding of possible cracking of the panel. Make a careful examination of this area. Under the bonnet, pay attention to the tool compartment. Over the years, rain gets into the compartment via the louvers and the rear hinge. This compartment is an area often neglected by owners and can be a site of hidden rust. While under the bonnet, check the firewall, in particular the lower half. This can be wood or metal depending on the model and receives water from above and below. A well-known site of rust is immediately above where the firewall joins the floor.

Now check the sidelights. The point where they are fixed to the top of the fenders is a weak place on all models and one that suffers stress. Check for cracking around the fitting point, and also check underneath the fenders to see if the supports have been reinforced with extra metal plates. These plates combined with filler can cover a multitude of faults.

The chassis is subjected to great stress and strains, and is constantly flexing. Check for cracks, plates or gussets welded to the chassis. If you find them, proceed with caution. You are now entering the realm of major expense. While checking the chassis, go along it tapping gently with the handle of a screwdriver or similar tool. This could well reveal thin points or even holes due to rust—the ringing note from the tapping will change if you hit on either. Perform the same test with a small magnet; all Morgan chassis are made of steel, and non-metal patches will reveal themselves. Check to see if the cross-members are cracked or broken, particularly where they join the chassis. Beware of the car on which the chassis and the underside of the floor and fenders are plastered with thick underseal; this again can cover a multitude of sins. A word of caution: since about 1970 the Morgan factory has offered under-sealing as an optional extra. This was never a thick application, never more than the thickness of a heavy coat of paint.

Small bubbles of rust may be found anywhere on the body panels, and in most cases they can be dealt with easily. They could be an indicator of something far more sinister, however, especially if the rust is coming through the panel rather than forming on top of it. These bubbles could indicate that water has been at work over a long period and that this section of the seasoned ash frame is now rotting. Rotting wood means that the body panels must be removed to renew the wood and are most likely rusted away like a saw edge, especially where the securing nails went through. Wherever possible, check all the wood frame with the point of a sharp knife or by tapping (rotten wood makes a dull thudding sound when tapped). Other clues to possible wood rot are dark stains or dark discoloration of the wood, especially at the joints. Except for the last few years, the factory did not preserve the wooden frame in any way. So if paint or creosote is on the frame anywhere, make an extra special examination.

Closely examine the door frames, as they are a major stress point for the wood and are also exposed to a lot of water. Yet another black spot to search for the dreaded rust and wood rot is the back panel. Remove the spare wheel, and inspect from every possible angle. You will find it difficult to do so, and that is the reason why you must persevere. If an area is hard for you to see, then it was hard for the previous owners to have maintained and cleaned.

If you find fiberglass fenders, they have been made by an outside company, never by the factory, except on the Plus 4 Plus, of course. Owners fit them as a cheap form of

accident repair or as a weight-reducing exercise for competition work. In either case, check for signs of damage, and also take special note of the condition of the engine and suspension. If you are inspecting a car with fiberglass fenders or are lucky enough to have found a Plus 4 Plus, remember that fiberglass produces a lot of its own special problems, such as cracking within the body shell, spider-web cracks in the paintwork and patches. With the Plus 4 Plus, the most important areas to check are where the body joins to the chassis. Morgan used bolts and pop rivets in the joining; wooden spacers were used at the rear. Cracked or broken fiberglass in these areas, or even rotted wood blocks, could mean having to strip down the whole body to be able to remove the affected area to work on—and this can be expensive.

When inspecting any used car with a view to purchase, check the paintwork for cracks, chips, scratches, fading and other problems. Repainting a Morgan is no big deal, but it does require the removal of the fenders, bonnet and doors if you do the job properly. There are no hard and fast rules about color. Normally, Morgans were painted in a single color, from a choice of about eight to ten, depending on the year of manufacture. Two-tone or special colors were used if the customer ordered it and was willing to pay extra for the privilege.

When checking the inside of the car, make sure you lift the carpets and check the floors for rust and wood rot. The same applies under the seats. The condition of the upholstery should be taken into consideration when negotiating with the seller, but upholstery is not too expensive to replace if necessary. Check all instruments, and note the mileage recorded on the odometer. Then look at the pedal rubbers because the amount of wear can be an indication of the correct odometer reading. Tonneau covers and hoods are easily made but are not interchangeable or capable of being bought off the shelf. They must be made to fit an individual car, no two cars being exactly the same.

As explained previously, Morgans are a hard, rough ride, and they are even worse if the shock absorbers and springs are weakened. This is a frequent fault to be found but not too expensive to put right. The ride also causes another common fault, this one in the unique front suspension sliding pillars. Wear can be readily noted, first by the amount of play in the steering (but this can also indicate wear in the steering box or linkage) and also by a small but distinct lateral movement of the front wheels if they are rocked sideways from the top.

Engines are less of a problem because most engines in four-wheelers are easily replaceable with reconditioned units. The exceptions to this are the Coventry Climax and Standard Special engines, which are almost unobtainable. Most British Ford engines were prone to leaking oil, but this did not always indicate a drastic problem. Nevertheless, it is advisable to check carefully. The drive chain, including the gearboxes, gives little or no trouble but examine the whole chain, and also note if the greasing points have been regularly lubricated.

Last, but by no means least, make sure you drive the car. Check that the brakes do not pull to the side, squeak or chatter. Listen for a clunking noise from the drive train or rear axle when you accelerate away from stop. If possible, lift your foot off the accelerator and listen for any whining sounds from the back axle.

Try to use your list of faults as possible bargaining points. More than likely, these will not have any effect at all on the seller, but they are good indicators of just how much work and expense you are getting involved in if you buy the car. Morgans are not so thick on the ground in the United States that you will be able to walk around the corner and view another. It all becomes a question of compromise—and a question of just how desperate you are to own a Morgan.

You will discover that the Morgan has never been a particularly complicated car, either in bodywork or mechanical detail. It therefore follows that armed with the right manual, most people can carry out much of the restoration work themselves. A large number of specialist firms will supply you with anything that you need to carry out the job properly. Should you feel that the work

is beyond you or that you have not got the time, there are yet again plenty of specialist firms for you, provided your bag of double eagles or greenbacks is large enough.

As for the model you choose, that is a personal decision between you and your bank manager. A three-wheeler is very much a plaything and completely impractical in this modern world—which is exactly the right reason for buying one. They are great fun. Four-wheelers present a wider choice. There are advocates for both the flat-radiator models and the cowled-radiator models. My personal preference is for the flat-radiator models, but because I already own one, my selection is biased. Plus 8s are fast and can be frustrating within the speed limit. As will be seen when you read on, the 4/4 models vary a great deal in performance depending on which model you choose. The Plus 4s incorporate every variation of model, including the highly sought after two- or four-seater drophead coupes. In the opinion of most enthusiasts, the ultimate Morgan is the Plus 4 Super Sports.

Bitsas

This is the appropriate place to insert a word of warning to all prospective Morgan three-wheeler buyers. Over the years, the simplicity of the Morgan's design has led to many cars being constructed from spare parts that have been carefully gathered together by enthusiasts. On many occasions where a particular part has been impossible to obtain, pieces from other models have been adapted to complete the project. These cars are known as bitsas. In addition, many replica bodies have been built on other model chassis. Over the years, these cars have gathered their very own history, and as the years progress and the number of owners increases, it becomes hard to know exactly if such a car is ex-works or not (see also the chapter on the Sports model). When considering buying a Morgan, by far the best thing to do is to gather together as many facts and numbers as possible and contact the Morgan Three-Wheeler Club registrar for further information.

Morgans in the United States and Canada

It was not until the mid-1950s that Americans really discovered the Morgan. It was a good thing that they did, as Peter Morgan will readily admit. If it had not been for the American market in the fifties and sixties, there can be little doubt that the Morgan Motor Company would have collapsed. For most of this period, nearly eighty-five percent of the company's total production was exported to the United States.

Even this market was not troublefree. In 1961, a great recession struck the California aircraft industry. Not only did it hit the prosperity of those immediately involved, but it also spread throughout the whole country, with a detrimental effect on all subsidiary companies. So badly did sports car sales drop that MG and Triumph agents were reduced to holding auction sales in an attempt to reduce their stocks. If it had not been for the timely intervention of Peter Morgan, when the Morgan New York agent canceled his entire shipment, the company could have been in serious trouble. It just so happened that Peter Morgan and his wife were taking a holiday in America when the cancellation was received at the factory. The factory cabled him at his hotel and informed him of the cancellation. Peter ordered that the shipment be sent and immediately went to New York to see if his personal intervention could improve things. His strategy worked; he persuaded the agent to accept delivery, and while he was there met a large number of American enthusiasts. All this helped to stimulate interest in the marque.

Nevertheless, back in England the factory's production had to be cut back by one car a week. This does not sound like much, but it did represent about fourteen percent of pro-

Extensive tests, supervised by the US Department of Transport, had to be carried out before Bill Fink obtained the necessary permissions and authorizations to import Morgans into the United States. *John H. Shealy II*

duction. Slowly the market improved, but it was to be almost two years before production and sales returned to their previous levels.

Several valuable lessons were learned from this episode. The two major ones were in the need to extend the company's markets to avoid ever again being too dependent on the sales to one country and the need for Peter Morgan to be available to visit enthusiasts of the marque around the world. Another event that affected the market at that time was the victory of a Morgan Plus 4 Lawrencetune Super Sports in its class at the Le Mans twenty-four-hour race in 1962. In addition, the introduction of a new model always helps to improve sales, especially if it is a startling one, and in 1968 the introduction of the Plus 8 was to have a dramatic impact on sales worldwide.

Although throughout the initial development of the Plus 8 everything was done to meet the new motor vehicle regulations introduced in the United States in the late 1960s, Morgan was forced to drop out of the market by the end of 1971. The main reason for this was the increasing standards required for exhaust emission control, which caused even Rover to leave the market. In addition, there were many other requirements such as 5 mph impact bumpers and seatbelt warning buzzers. Although all these changes would eventually become available to Morgan as they were introduced by the major manufacturers, there would always be a delay. This was because changes were always introduced at the latest date required by the new legislation. Then, of course, a long delay ensued before they were adapted for use by Morgan, thus creating long gaps in export production, gaps that would be far from financially acceptable to the company and car buyers.

When the supply of Morgans to the United States stopped, American enthusiast Bill Fink, who from 1969 had traded in Morgan parts, repairs and the sale of secondhand Morgans, was determined to find a way to import them. From the enquiries he made of the Transportation Department and all the other relevant governmental departments, he discovered that any car powered by propane gas was exempt from the emission control regulations. Having successfully overcome the most serious of all the legal requirements, he set about investigating ways to overcome the remainder. He worked out that if the factory made some of the modifications during construction, he would be able to complete the work in the United States and get each car acceptable for resale. In 1973, he was in a position to approach Peter Morgan, who eventually agreed with Fink's basic ideas and promised to supply him with up to twenty-four cars a year, providing Fink could obtain all the necessary permissions and could sell the end result, so proving that the scheme worked. Due to

Imported Morgans undergo modifications and conversion to propane gas power at Bill Fink's San Francisco garage. *Roger Moran*

bureaucratic delays, Fink did not sell his first car until 1976.

For these imported cars, some of the work is carried out at the factory: telescopic gas-filled shock absorbers mounted behind reinforced front and rear bumpers to comply with the 5 mph head and tail-end crash test legislation, four-seater-size windscreens and a special steel reinforcing hoop or band bolted to the chassis behind the dashboard. On arrival in the United States, steel beams are fitted into the doors to meet the side impact regulations. In addition, rear roll-over bars, inertia-reel seatbelts, padded sun visors and seatbelt warning alarms are all fitted by Fink, and then the interior is coated with a flameproof fluid. The conversion of the engine requires a special eighteen-gallon fuel tank with the filler valve neatly hidden under the spare-wheel mounting, sealed fuel lines, and a vaporizer and a lock-off to stop the supply when the engine is switched off. The inlet manifold and carburetors are changed. Finally, a forty-five page dossier with full written and photographic evidence of all the modifications carried out has to be prepared for each car.

In 1986, another American enthusiast, Win Sharples from Virginia, successfully obtained permission to import Morgans into the United States and was granted an agency by the Morgan Motor Company. All the modifications listed above are carried out by his company as well.

In Canada, the exhaust emission control laws are not as strict as in the United States, and as a result, the fuel-injected Ford XR3 and the Rover engines both comply with regulations. Carburetor versions, however, do not burn fuel so cleanly or as completely as the injection engines and therefore cannot be used. All other modifications do apply and all imported new Morgans must be modified by the authorized Canadian distributor before permission is granted for them to be sold.

New Morgans can now be purchased in either the United States or Canada. The extensive modifications necessary will always mean that the numbers will never again approach those of the 1950s or 1960s. The question of whether to buy a new or second-hand example must be up to the individual and must depend on many factors.

Investment ratings

A few, and only a few, true investors are to be found in Morgans. The serious normally invest in the world of Rolls-Royce, Bentley, Bugatti, Porsche and so on. Those who have ventured into Morgans have soon discovered that no matter how thick-skinned they thought they were, they too fall for the fascination of this living antique. And then they just cannot part with their Morgan. Providing you are sensible and have not paid a ridiculous price for your car, it is rare for Morgan owners to lose money if they are forced into selling.

All Morgans have been the "in" car for many years. Obviously, some models are more desirable than others. There is little or no doubt that, with the possible exception of cars less than four years old, all will increase in value. Unlike other marques, the star rating is therefore used in this book as an indicator for the most desirable models, rather than for their investment potential.

Condition is obviously a factor in buying any car, but with Morgans it is not such a governing factor. When you are contemplating buying a Morgan, remember that its production was like that of no other car in the world. Any prospective buyer must realize that normal production figures do not apply to Morgans. This can best be illustrated by using the example of arguably the most desirable of all four-wheeled Morgans, the Plus 4 Super Sports. The total number of this model produced over seven years was only 104 or 113, depending on which inter-pretation one places on the works' records. This is less than a week's production for a rarer mass-produced car. It therefore follows that a concours condition example is in the five-star most desirable category, and its price would reflect this. However, to be lucky enough to find one of the previously untraced examples of this model, no matter in what condition, is always a true Morgan enthusiast's dream, and such a find must therefore rate a five-star listing. Obviously, the price would follow the condition, but could still be well in excess of a three-star example of another model.

★★★★★ Most desirable and already expensive (but will continue to appreciate in value), these normally are sold between Morgan enthusiasts and are rarely advertised outside club publications. The better the condition, the higher the price.

★★★★ Still very desirable but not so rare as the five-star listings, these Morgans are more affordable. Condition must be far more of a consideration.

★★★ Good examples of most models represent good value and can only appreciate in value if the condition is maintained.

★★ This category includes any example that can be purchased and driven, but lacks rarity, and is of only average or below average condition. The cost of restoring should only just match the car's value afterward, unless the purchaser carries out the majority of the work.

★ These cars are any Morgan (other than a rare model) that only a true enthusiast would buy, including a rusting, rotting hulk that would cost far more to restore than it would ever be worth. In the Morgan world even these examples have purchasers waiting and command far more money than could be thought possible.

A note on engine numbers

While dealing with numbers to be found on Morgans, a brief explanation is necessary as to why the engine numbers on Morgans do not follow in sequence. The Morgan Motor Company has always purchased engines from outside manufacturers, and so deliveries are made as stocks are running low. The delivery of twenty, thirty or forty engines is made and their numbers are more than likely consecutive, but when unloaded, they are placed in front of the remaining stock from the previous delivery, and not necessarily in order.

When an engine is required, the first in line is invariably taken, and time is not wasted checking the sequence. Eventually all stock is used, but the sequence of the engine numbers in the cars apparently has no logical progression and does not correspond to the sequence in which the cars were manufactured.

Chapter 1

Morgan Runabout

When Henry Frederick Stanley Morgan purchased an Eagle Tandem 8 hp three-wheeler in 1901, he little dreamed that it would lead him into becoming one of the world's major three-wheeler cyclecar manufacturers. The Eagle was fitted with a motorcycle-type rear wheel and a conventional car-type front axle. Between the front wheels was a padded seat for the passenger. In 1906, H.F.S., as he was to become known to his friends and throughout the motoring world, left the Great Western Railway where he worked as a draftsman and went into partnership with a close friend. They opened a garage in Malvern, Worcestershire. The venture flourished, and H.F.S. turned his thoughts to making a car of his own: a vehicle that would be a cross between a motorcycle and a car. Not a motorcycle, but a cyclecar.

"It went like a rocket," was a comment often heard about a Morgan three-wheeler, and so it should have done when one considers the assistance given to H.F.S. in 1908–09 by a certain W. Stephenson-Peach, the engineering master of Malvern College. Stephenson-Peach was a direct descendant of George Stephenson, the locomotive pioneer and designer of the famous Rocket locomotive. Without this help, the Morgan Motor Company Limited might have never existed. By enlisting the engineering expertise of Stephenson-Peach and combining it with his own engineering skills, Morgan used the college machinery to construct his prototype single-seater three-wheeled car.

The Morgan was not the first three-wheeler; numerous tandem-seated tri-cycles preceded it. However, H.F.S. Morgan's was probably the first three-wheeler to have the engine fitted in front like a car, independent wheel springing and a ridged frame—a configuration that was to prove to be the right one. H.F.S. must be regarded as the pioneer and father of the three-wheeler cyclecar.

The Standard model 1910-28	

"A three-wheeled runabout which should on no account be missed by visitors to the show is the Morgan in the annexe." This is how one motorcycling magazine referred to H.F.S. Morgan's first exhibition of his recently developed three-wheeler on stand number 250 at the Olympia Motor Cycle Show in 1910.

H.F.S. displayed two versions of the car, one fitted with a 4 hp JAP 85.5 mm x 85 mm single-cylinder engine and the other with a twin-cylinder 8 hp version of the same engine. Both cars were single-seaters and were fitted with tiller steering.

By 1911, H.F.S. had designed and built a prototype two-seater version of the car. In this the driver and the passenger sat side-by-side, and the car was still fitted with tiller steering. The body was sparse and was not fitted with mudguards. The registration number was CJ 743.

This was the same registration number that appeared on the car that H.F.S. drove on the Auto Cycle Union (A.C.U.) Six Day Trial later in the year, and by this time the car was fitted with a full body, including the open-fronted coal-scuttle bonnet that was to become so familiar. In addition, acetylene lamps, mudguards and steering wheel were fitted. In June 1912, H.F.S. married Hilda Ruth Day, and this was the car in which they toured Wales on their honeymoon.

This car was also fitted with a three-speed gearbox, as opposed to the two-speed box used in normal production cars. It was suggested by a motoring journalist of the time that the three-speed gearbox may have been one that was originally to have been used in a proposed Morgan motorcycle, but this is the only reference that I have ever found on the subject. In 1913, however, a four-speed gearbox was offered by the factory as an optional extra for £10. This was made by fitting an additional two-speed gearbox behind the clutch and brazing it to the tube

that enclosed the propeller shaft. The gears were large-spur type. The standard two-speed gearbox was also provided in the bevel box. Thus, four speeds in all were provided, and the alteration to the chassis necessary to fit this arrangement was slight. The gears were operated by a small lever situated between the driver and the passenger, and the standard gear lever on the off-side was still retained. This meant that it was necessary at times to operate both levers simultaneously when changing into top or bottom gear.

By 1913, a Commercial Carrier version of the Standard model was on offer. Designed for the "conveyance of small parcels," the carrying space was created by fitting a container over the tail, from the rear of the seats. The carrier was hinged up to give access to the rear wheel and could be removed completely by unscrewing eight nuts; this restored the vehicle to its original passenger status. The cost ready for the road was £95 plus £3 extra for the alternative body. It was advertised as being able to carry loads up to 196 lb. but according to contemporary reports, weights in the region of 125 lb. was a far more realistic figure.

The Standard model was withdrawn from the catalog for 1915, with only the Sporting,

The 1910 Olympia Motor Cycle Show was the first public showing of the new Morgan Runabout. Fitted with a 4 hp JAP air-cooled engine and only a little over two feet high, it left some motoring writers wondering if "it might, with its present sized wheels prove unsuitable for use in districts where the roads are very rough." How wrong could they be? Tiller steering was standard, but wheel steering was available at extra charge.

This prototype with its sparse bodywork still retained tiller steering. However, by the 1911 Olympia Show, Morgan had greatly improved the body design. *Morgan Motor Company*

Grand Prix and De Luxe models available, the latter earning the title by having a door.

When announced at the 1921 Olympia Show, the New Standard Popular model was introduced as if it was a completely new model, but it was a reintroduction of the Standard model first introduced in 1911. For many years, some people believed the name included a pun on the word "popular," which they thought referred to the use of black popular in the construction of the bodywork; the wood was believed to have been imported from France by a local timber merchant and then supplied to the Morgan factory. However, as Peter Morgan pointed out to me a few years ago, popular would have been too soft for bodywork, and the most likely timber used would have been American whitewood. Priced at £150, the car was a short wheelbase model that came complete with acetylene lamps, hood, windscreen, license holder, tools and an oil can. Morgan offered it with either a 10 hp Blackburn or 8 hp JAP air-cooled engine, and it weighed 532 lb.

The year 1923 saw the introduction of front wheel brakes as an optional extra, at a cost of £6, but the motoring press only con-sidered them necessary in an emergency. The Morgan works had experimented for over two years before perfecting the idea. The drums were made integral with the hubs of the wire wheels, and attached to the pivoting axles were pairs of friction-faced internal-expanding shoes worked by a cam. They were operated by a substantial Bowden cable from a hand-operated lever, and compensation for equal braking on both wheels was by the Bowden principle as well.

The timing of the introduction was perfect, as it immediately negated any advantage Austin may have gained by introducing them on their 7 series models, the Tourer or Chummy, either of which cost £165. By this time, the Standard Popular price had dropped to £128. The battle to sell motor vehicles as the postwar depression took hold was intense. All manufacturers of motorcars and motorcycles slowly cut their profit margins to the bare minimum in an attempt to attract trade. Morgan not only cut its prices but also continued to make improvements on its product. By 1925, the price of the Standard Popular model had been reduced to £110, and it could be supplied with electric lamps to replace acetylene ones, at an extra cost of

The Commercial Carrier version of the Standard model was introduced in 1913. The easy fitting and removal of the carrier body meant that the owner could use the same vehicle for both business and pleasure. *Morgan Motor Company*

£8. In addition, for those customers wanting the last word in Morgan luxury, an electric starter could be fitted at an extra cost of £12.

At the 1925 Olympia Show, Morgan announced that electric lighting was now standard on all its models, but in an effort to keep down the price of the lowest-priced car in its range, the Standard was the only one not fitted with an electric horn.

By 1926, the model had gained both an electric horn and a double windscreen as standard, at a price that had dropped to £89, which was still way below the price of an Austin 7. The model continued production until 1928, was slowly phased out during that year and was not listed for 1929. The Standard model was not to go into production ever again.

Prospects

This model commands a good price when the few examples that survive ever come onto the market. However, it is not the model that investors look at with too much interest. The Standard is mainly sold among enthusiasts.

Grand Prix 1913-26	★★★★★

The Grand Prix model came about purely as a result of Morgan's competition successes. In the summer of 1913, the first Cycle Car Grand Prix of France was held at Amiens. This was an important event to cyclecar manufacturers from all over Britain and Europe. H.F.S. had already established that sales success came through competition success. Three Morgans were designed and prepared for the race, and because they were competition cars they were not all exactly alike. The one thing that they did have in common was that they were wider and longer than the Standard model. One of these cars was driven by W. G. McMinnies, a member of the editorial staff of the new *Cyclecar* magazine and his riding mechanic was Frank Thomas, the honorary secretary of the Cycle Car Club. At an average speed of 42 mph, McMinnies romped home to win the event.

Immediately, the Morgan Motor Company advertised that it would supply exact copies of McMinnies' car at a cost of £115. At the Motor Cycle Show in November of the same year, the Morgan stand featured three versions of the Grand Prix model. Versions one and two were offered at a cost of £105 and were fitted with side-valve JAP engines. Both were two-seaters, but one was narrower than the other. Version three was fitted with an overhead-valve water-cooled JAP engine and was identical in every way to the actual race car. According to the catalog, the car had proved itself capable of sustained

The New Standard Popular model was reintroduced in 1921. Starting with the 1926 models, electric lighting was standard on all models. Also standard for the Standard model was the

double windscreen. Front wheel brakes were still an optional extra and were not fitted to this example. *D. Rushton and Morgan Motor Company*

speeds in excess of 60 mph and was priced at £115.

The Morgan staff manning the stand at the show could hardly keep pace with the orders that they were receiving. Within days they had taken orders for nearly the whole of the following year's production, including 150 for export, not surprisingly to France.

Although Morgans were produced in limited numbers through World War One, any further development of this or any other model during this period that may have been considered was ended in 1917 when a ministry priority certificate became necessary for the production, except under War Office contract, of any motor vehicle. In spite of this requirement, motoring magazines gave details of the various models in the Morgan range throughout the war. However, from 1917 all reports ended with the following words: "It must be distinctly understood that no new model can be supplied at the present time except under Ministry of Munitions Priority Certificates."

The Grand Prix model was phased out at the end of 1926, when demand for it was overtaken by that for the Aero model. Without doubt the Grand Prix was the sportiest Morgan produced during this period; its design did not alter much throughout the years of its production. It was always offered with a choice of engine: in alphabetical order, these were the Anzani, Baker Precision, Blackburn, JAP (by far the largest number) and MAG.

If it had not been for World War One, 1914 could have seen the introduction of a new model. It was the outbreak of the war that caused the cancellation of the projected first Isle of Man Tourist Trophy Light Car Race. H.F.S. had been determined to add this event to his list of triumphs, and he had designed a special racing car just for the event.

This car was based on a lengthened Grand Prix chassis, which was necessary to lower the seats so that they were about 4½ inches above the ground, with the torque tube passing between them. This design had the effect of lowering the center of gravity and so greatly improving the already exceptional road-holding capabilities of the Runabout.

True to the maxim that Competition Success sold Morgans, the company used this advertisement to announce the availability of "Front Wheel Brakes" in 1923. Several years passed before they were adopted as standard on all models.

Morgan prepared three experimental cars for the first Motor Cycle Grand Prix of France in 1913. This is one of the two cars fitted with air-cooled side-valve JAP engines. The third car, fitted with a water-cooled JAP, won the race. *Morgan Motor Company*

This was especially necessary for the twisting roads to be used for the race. The back forks were widened, and a larger brake drum fitted. The usual two-speed gearbox was fitted with 3.33:1 and 5.25:1 ratios, which gave terrific acceleration. The sparse bodywork was made entirely of wood with a pointed front, incorporating a tool box, and ended immediately behind the engine.

The large cylindrical six-gallon fuel tank was mounted across the body immediately behind the seats and had a rod through its center, which was used to secure the body side-members. The petrol was pressure fed to an Amal carburetor that possessed a very large float chamber. The pressure was maintained by a pump mounted on the dashboard.

This lightweight vehicle was powered by a special racing eight-valve air-cooled V-twin MAG engine. The cylinder heads were detachable and were machined out inside. Each had two inlet and two exhaust valves and they were operated by long tappet rods, which were provided with adjusters. The rocker arms were fitted with screw-up greasers and long coil springs of different sizes for inlet and exhaust. The bevel drive to the magneto was enclosed. The engine had a high compression ratio and developed about 30 hp, and would travel at 50–60 mph at one-third throttle. This was yet another Morgan that carried the works' registration number CJ 743, which appeared on several different models. This special racing car was never developed because of the wartime restrictions.

Prospects

Collectors regard the Grand Prix model as one of the most desirable of the three-wheelers. It therefore commands a high price if one ever comes onto the market.

The outstanding success of the three competition Morgans in France led to the immediate introduction of the Grand Prix model. This 1914 example is a JAP air-cooled side-valve production model. *D. Rushton*

This beautifully restored Grand Prix belongs to Chris Booth, the well-known Morgan three-wheeler expert, who runs the only museum in the world devoted to Morgans. *Chris Booth*

The 1914 Auto Cycle Union Six Day Trial. This Standard model was being driven by Billie Jones. *D. Rushton*

Due to the war, few changes were made to the Standard model, as can clearly be seen in this 1918 catalog photograph. The wheel discs were supplied as an optional extra. The body-mounted canister was the acetylene and water container that supplied the gas for the lighting. The model was fitted with a water-cooled JAP engine and cost £137. *D. Rushton*

The model that never was! H.F.S. Morgan and his wife Ruth in the 1914 TT racer at Stile Kop. It is interesting to note that there is little tread on the front wheel tires but almost a "knobbly" on the rear drive wheel. Note also the height of the seats above the ground, sparse bodywork and the body sides securing rod that passed through the rear-mounted fuel tank. *Morgan Motor Company*

By 1913, the Morgan Motor Company was offering three models for sale: the Standard Runabout, the Sporting, and the De Luxe, the latter two being no more than variants of the Runabout, with certain body or engine modifications. The Sporting model was fitted with a more enclosed body, which meant that the occupants had to step over the sides into the car, rather than stepping into it through the open sides. The De Luxe model had a much more enveloping body and was supplied with a door to facilitate entrance. *D. Rushton*

Immediately after the war, the De Luxe and the Sporting models underwent several improvements. The De Luxe received the majority: a revised fascia that included a small "recess for gloves, etc," wire netting covering in place of the rear louvers in the bonnet sides and the option of an air-cooled MAG engine (£135) or a water-cooled JAP engine (£145). The Sporting model was only available with the air-cooled MAG engine (£130), and its body was similar to the De Luxe but without the door.

Family four-seater 1917-37	★★★
Sports Family 1931-36	★★★★
Family De Luxe 1930-32	★★★★

The Family model, which was to become so popular in the twenties, was first experimented with in 1912, when a prototype was built on a remarkably long chassis. In 1914, the factory built the first experimental four-wheeled Morgan fitted with a four-seater body. It was powered by a Dorman engine but was never developed further, although it was patented. It is interesting to contemplate what might have happened to the development of the Morgan Motor Company had not war been declared later in the same year, but as it has been described, this stopped any further experiments in that direction.

Although part of the factory was made over to the production of shells and other types of munitions and over half the work force was away at the war, Morgan still maintained limited production. As a result of the war work, H.F.S. was able to purchase new machinery with the aid of government grants and the fixed profits imposed on all munitions contractors.

The first four-seater production model was announced in 1917, and by late 1918, H.F.S.—along with his wife, daughter and three other toddlers who were borrowed for the occasion—was pictured in a four-seater for advertising purposes. In 1919, E. B. Ware, the head of the experimental department of JAP engines and who was to become a leading Morgan racer, was pictured with his wife and family in an example that was fitted with an experimental 8 hp engine (which was to become standard for the model) and a wedged shape oil and petrol tank, which was so designed to aid airflow.

This 1917 experimental four-seater paved the way to the final design of one of the most suc- cessful models produced by Morgan. *Morgan Motor Company*

This four-seater had an advertised weight of 532 lb.

In November 1919, weekly production rose to forty to fifty cars of all models, and the four-seater first made its appearance to the motoring public at the 1919 Olympia Show, when the 1920 models were announced and the four-seater model was named the Family model. The model was fitted with an adjustable front seat to increase legroom should an adult be carried in the back. The car was advertised as being able to carry three adults or two adults and two children, but at that time no claims were made about comfort.

Throughout the 1920s, this model led Morgan's fight in the war against small cheap four-wheeled cars like the Austin 7 or the motorcycle-sidecar combinations, both of which could carry two adults and two children or three adults. Of course, all other Morgan models were in the same war, but it was the Family model that spearheaded Morgan's attack. The model was extremely popular and was to be in great demand right into the thirties.

The model was supplied mainly with air- or water-cooled side-valve JAP engines, although a few were fitted with other special-order engines. Wheel spoke covering discs were also offered as an extra, at a charge of £3. By 1926, the height of the sides of this model had been increased by one inch, and double windscreens were fitted.

In 1927, the model was supplied with seven-inch front wheel brakes as standard. Yet problems arose. "The question of brakes is a ticklish one. If they are weak the owner complains bitterly, and if they are too pow-

This clever 1925 advertisement clearly illustrates the attempts made to arouse the latent speed tendencies in the family man by placing the record-breaking achievements of Harold Beart alongside the illustration of the Family model.

This beautifully restored 1928 Family model shows the upright double windscreen. The top half could be opened outwards for ventilation. The model was also fitted with electric lighting; however, in an effort to trim costs and therefore keep the price of the model competitive, Morgan still supplied a manually operated horn. *John H. Sheally II*

erful he may get into trouble through over-eager application. The expert can be given powerful brakes, because he knows how to use them, but the novice must be catered for. Those on the Family Morgan were adequate, and no more, though the front ones could have had more bite with perfect safety." So wrote the correspondent in *The Motor Cycle* magazine of June 5, 1930, in his review of the 980 cc Family Morgan. The review ended with these words: "Having praised and criticised where necessary, and treating the Family Morgan as a vehicle pure and simple, it is rather a surprise to remember its price. It is simplicity itself, is easy to handle, and provides a standard of comfort almost on a par with that of the small four-wheeler—with a far better performance on hills under full load." Its price at the time was £97.10, including lighting, starter, speedometer and sidescreens.

Also available for the 1929 models was the reintroduced Commercial Carrier bolt-on body, as supplied in 1913 for the Standard model. This Carrier body was fitted over the rear seats from the back of the front seats. As a motoring journalist of the period wrote, "a business vehicle during the week, and a pleasure car on Sundays, combined in the same machine, is something many people desire."

In 1931, the Family model appeared with what Morgan claimed was a redesigned body, although it was basically just revamped: the windscreen sloped, the engine cowl was lowered and the bonnet was slightly longer. Also fitted were cycle-type front fenders. This "new" body did not immediately replace the previous one and was confined almost exclusively to the Family De Luxe model. It was also possible to still buy the 1930 style body in 1931 at a reduced price. All these models were fitted with a two-speed gearbox only, and this version was still on offer right up to the end of 1933.

In 1931, a new model designated the Sports Family was introduced. It was built with the De Luxe specifications and a two-seater body, complete with split windscreen and exposed engine. It was not fitted with the Family enveloping bonnet.

The prototype of the redesigned 1931 body reveals the "improvements." The windscreen was slanted, the engine cowl lowered and the bonnet longer, and the car has cycle-type fenders. These changes were confined to the Family De Luxe model. This photograph was staged for advertising purposes; the driver was Harry Jones, a director of Morgan, and the passengers were all members of the company's office staff. *Morgan Motor Company*

This 1934 model was newly fitted with Dunlop Magna detachable wheels, with the spare carried at the rear. The windscreen was once again a one-piece but still retained the slope introduced in 1931. The door handles were moved to outside the much enlarged doors. *D. Rushton*

The 1932 models showed major changes. First, the new three-speed and reverse gearbox was fitted, and second, the sixty-degree JAP coil ignition engines were fitted. Next, the model was offered in a two-seater or a four-seater version, the latter having a large luggage compartment in the tail. The Sports Family was also available with the LTOWZ JAP overhead-valve water-cooled engine, and it could now carry three adults or two adults and two children.

The introduction of the three-speed gearbox also led to a true redesign of the bodywork. In 1933, the body was fitted with two large opening doors and a square-shaped tail panel, on which was mounted a spare wheel. Besides the usual offering of the air- or water-cooled side-valve JAP engines, a few cars were fitted with the new Matchless MX side-valve water-cooled engine. This engine

was to prove to be popular, and from 1935 the Family model was fitted with the Matchless MX engine up until its production ceased in 1937. The use of the Matchless engine meant the radiator header tank had to be altered to enable it to hold more coolant and for better air circulation around the core. At the same time, the Family and the Sports Family models were fitted with the round barrel-back tails, which stayed until the end of production.

For the 1934 and 1935 seasons Morgan offered the Sports Family with a choice of four engines: the side- or overhead-valve water-cooled JAP, the overhead-valve air-cooled Matchless MX2 or the side-valve water-cooled Matchless MX. In 1936 when the model was phased out, the choice was three: the Matchless MX, the MX2 or the MX4 water-cooled overhead-valve engine.

Prospects

The Family model was most likely the largest production three-wheeler model made by Morgan. They are not as sought after as may be thought but are still a car that fetches good prices in the open market. The Sports Family is of course regarded as being more desirable, mainly because of its better performance and also because it is so much rarer than the ordinary Family model.

This posed photograph for the introduction of the new three-speed gearbox in 1932 shows just how much room there really was in the Family model. The back seats were narrower than the front, and of course the ride was bumpy to say the least because the passengers were seated immediately over the top of the rear wheel. It was also drafty because the seats were higher to clear the rear wheel and had no sidescreens for protection when the hood was down. *Morgan Motor Company*

The 1934-35 Sports Family model was powered by a water-cooled side-valve Matchless MX engine. It was also available with side- or overhead-valve water-cooled JAP or overhead-valve air-cooled Matchless MX2 engines. *D. Rushton*

Sports Family 1935 three-speed

Engine	Overhead-valve, Matchless 50 degree V-twin, bore and stroke 85.5 mm, 990 cc, detachable cylinder heads, Lo-ex pistons, forked connecting rods, roller-bearing big ends, fully floating gudgeon pins, enclosed rockers with positive lubrication, water-cooled
Ignition	Lucas coil
Carburetor	Amal motorcycle type
Lubrication	Dry sump, one-gal oil tank
Gearbox	Morgan three-speed
Transmission	Single dry plate clutch
Suspension	Front: independent vertical enclosed helical springs with shock absorbers, rear: underslung steel quarter-elliptic springs
Brakes	Internal expanding, cable operated
Wheels	18x3 in. Dunlop Magna, spare wheel on rear panel removable to give access to rear forks
Tires	Dunlop
Dimensions	Overall length 126 in., overall width 59 in., wheelbase 87 in., track 50 in., ground clearance 6½ in.
Weight	966 lb. completely equipped and with full tanks
Bodywork	Sheet metal and wood, coachbuilt, safety glass windscreen with Lucas pneumatic wiper
Lamps	Electric set, 8 in. headlights
Electrics	Electric starter. Horn operated by button on dash. Ignition switch, lamp and dynamo switch, ammeter, ignition warning light and speedometer
Price	£95 including hood, £3.10s for non-standard finish

These advertisements of 1931 and 1935 paraded the psychology that the company was still using on the family man: "inside every man there is a potential Boy Racer trying to get out." Although the 1935 advertisement illustrated the F2 model, the catalog and background still played on the passions of the sports car family man.

Morgan Motor Company built one or two prototypes of the Delivery van in 1928 or 1929, but it was not introduced as a production model until it was announced in 1933 for the 1934 season. Built on a Family model chassis, the Delivery van was to be the only enclosed three-wheeler Morgan ever to be built. The company had been producing a

pickup-style body in various forms from 1911, but this was its answer to the BSA and Raleigh three-wheeler vans that were introduced about this time. Strangely, this was a battle that Morgan did not win; the model was not at all popular, and few were sold. Quite a few examples of both the BSA and Raleigh vans still survive today, a fact that reflects the numbers originally sold. As far as is known, no original example of the Morgan van exists today, although in 1982 one was allegedly discovered in Paris, but nothing more has ever been heard about it. I am given to understand from the British Morgan Three-Wheeler Club that one or two members are in the process of constructing replicas of this model.

Prospects

Although the Delivery van does not convey the accepted image of a Morgan sports car, it is an important part of the company's production history. Therefore, the discovery of an original example could represent a good investment.

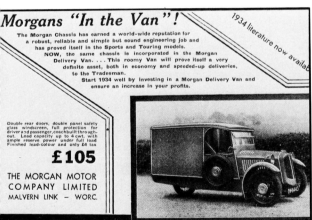

The prototype van was produced in 1928-29 and fitted on the Family model chassis. The roof has a distinct slope to the rear, and two doors open at the front. However, when production started in 1933, the roof had been squared off level at the rear and the bonnet was longer. By 1933, the van had the three-speed gearbox, Dunlop Magna detachable wheels and only one opening front door because the spare wheel was mounted on the other.

Delivery van	
Engine	Water-cooled 50 degree V-twin
Chassis	Layout as for Morgan three-wheeler passenger vehicles
Bodywork	Coachbuilt. "Exceptionally sturdy and undoubtedly the most pleasing body on a £4 tax machine." Double rear doors and double panel safety glass windscreen gave full protection for driver and passenger
Finish	Lead color paintwork
Load capacity	Maximum 448 lb.
Overall dimensions	Length 123 in., height 60 in., width 58 in.
Price	£105

Although Morgan announced the Aero model in November 1920 at the Motor Cycle Show at Olympia as a new model, strictly speaking this was not correct. In 1916, a cross between the Grand Prix and the Sporting model was produced. The car was fitted with a MAG water-cooled engine. The fenders curved straight down from the wheels, and the running board was connected to the fender. This removed the gap that had always run between the fender and the running board. The seats were lower than on the Grand Prix model and were also staggered, allowing more legroom. No windscreen or hood were provided, as it was believed that the sloping bonnet would divert the wind over the occupants.

Few of this model were produced due to the wartime restrictions, and it was never allocated a model designation name. When one compares this 1916 model with the Aero, there can be little doubt that this was in fact the Aero's prototype. The most famous people to purchase prototypes were Captain Albert Ball, V.C., D.S.O., M.C., who was certainly Britain's World War One greatest air ace, with over forty kills to his credit, and another fighter ace, Captain "Mad Jack" Woodhouse, M.C.

The Aero model was announced at the 1919 show but was not listed in the 1920 catalog, which stated that "owing to difficulties of production we have dropped the 'Family' and 'Aero' models." It was not until the 1920 show that the model was really in production and recognized by the motoring world.

The Aero model was fitted with two small, almost half-round, wind deflectors, which are known as Aero-screens. These screens were known at the time as aeroplane-type adjustable shields and remained fitted as standard to the Aero model until the 1930 model was introduced, when they were replaced by the two panel V-screen. The car

was also fitted with a tapering tail, plus a V-fronted air deflector under the bonnet tank and behind the radiator. An ingenious arrangement of cables linked to the Binks carburetor, allowed the throttle to be operated either by foot or by hand controls. The model was offered with a choice of MAG or JAP engines. In keeping with the rest of the Morgan range, front-wheel brakes were offered as an option at the extra cost of £6.

From mid-1923, the body styling changed. The holes leading to the V-fronted air deflectors under the bonnet tank were filled in with two flat panels that had six louvers cut into each one. The side panels were slightly shaped around the cockpit before continuing in a flat taper to the tail, where both sides met in a slightly rounded end. The bottom of the tail panel came up in almost a straight line until it was just below the level of the rear wheel. The top panel remained flat and almost horizontal. Other modifications included rounding the front fenders to follow the curve of the wheels, with the fender bottoms sweeping back and up until they were almost parallel to the ground. A snake's head horn was mounted on top of the off-side mudguard, and its long tube trailed to a rubber bulb fitted to the outside of the bodywork on the cockpit close to the steering wheel. In addition, two boat-type ventilators were fitted on the top of the bonnet, each one just in front of the V-screens. The gear and brake levers had been moved back and outside the bodywork, making it necessary for the driver to reach down and behind to operate them.

In 1924, the Aero was offered with a 1096 cc racing Blackburn overhead-valve water-cooled engine that lifted the speed of the car from the 60 mph capable with the Anzani engine to 70 mph. By 1925, the snake's head horn had been replaced by a much smaller and far more practical one mounted on the scuttle immediately between the Aero-screens. Moseley Float-on-Air cushions were fitted as standard.

The dashboard (or fascia) was polished aluminum (this was changed to mottled aluminum in 1929) and contained a Lucas ignition switchboard with an ammeter to the left in front of the passenger seat. A Best

In 1923, the Aero model underwent many body styling changes, including a snake's head horn and two boat-type ventilators. In addition, in 1924 the engine was changed to a 1096 cc racing Blackburn overhead-valve water-cooled engine. All the body "refinements" were not necessarily appreciated by all owners. This owner has made many alterations: note the blanked-off ventilator holes, the clip still on the side of the body where the reed and bulb section of the snake's head horn was fitted and the filled-in section between the Aero-screens. The owner has also fitted sidelights on the fenders. It is worthwhile to know that no production Morgan three-wheeler, no matter which model, was fitted with sidelights; however, some were fitted if especially ordered, but these are rare indeed. *D. Rushton*

& Lloyd drip-feed lubrication and pump complete with sight glass was mounted in the center of the board. A Watford magnetic speedometer was sighted immediately in front of the driver and could be easily seen through the steering wheel. The wheels were fitted with 26x3.5 inch straight-sided Dunlop Cord tires. The Lucas six-volt battery was fitted on a small platform on the off-side of the body, while on the near-side was a cast metal step in the shape of a letter M.

When the 1926 models were announced in November 1925, Morgan offered a new engine for the Aero. This was an overhead-valve water-cooled JAP type LTOW which when fitted with domed pistons produced more power than the Blackburn engine, which by this stage had become standard. In addition, the curved fenders had been changed to inclined flat ones, which had a small downward lip at the front to stop spray. A hood now available for the Aero cost an extra £3.

In October 1926 at the Olympia show, the company introduced another new model to the Aero range. This was the Aero Family with an LTOW JAP engine. To accommodate the two small extra seats, the wheelbase was extended four inches. As the motoring press stated, "the additional space could be occupied by children or filled with luggage when two grown-ups undertake an extended tour." The prototype of this model had been built earlier in the year, and a few examples had been sent out to Morgan's main agents before the show. In fact, on September 11 the Morgan agent in Sheffield, Freddie James, competed in one in the Hallamshire M.C. & L.C.C. Inter Team Trial.

By 1927, the model was fitted with 2:1 ratio steering as opposed to the direct method previously used. Also at this time, the bulb horn was replaced by an electrical one, and the operating button was located on the dashboard immediately under the oil drip-feed sight glass.

When the 1928 models were announced, a new version of the Aero was included. This was the Super Sports Aero. This name was soon to be shortened to Super Sports. The width of the bodywork for this new model was increased by six inches and the frame lowered by 2½ inches. The rear-end style had an entirely enclosed rear wheel above the axle and cycle-type mudguards. This arrangement was soon to become known as the beetle-back. Speeds in excess of 80 mph were claimed for the car.

In November 1929, a new type chassis was introduced; it was named the M chassis. The new chassis meant that the rear suspension was now underslung and a knock-out spindle allowed for easy removal of the back wheel. The foot brake was the internal expanding type, arranged inside the low gear sprocket and operated by a flexible cable from the pedal. This meant that the bevel box could be redesigned, with its two forged-steel wheel-supports being arranged co-axially with the countershaft. This enabled the whole of the rear mechanism to be removed as one unit. In addition, the new layout meant that it was now possible to house the battery in a locker concealed behind the seat squab (an easily detachable cushion which formed the seat's backrest). The new arrangement reduced the chassis length by three inches, leaving the body dimensions unchanged.

H.F.S. Morgan and his wife Ruth in a Blackburn-engined Aero compete in the Birmingham/Holyhead/Birmingham 24 hour trial. *D. Rushton*

In October 1926, the Aero Family model was introduced, with an LTOW JAP engine. The wheelbase was increased by four inches to accommodate the two extra seats. *D. Rushton*

In February 1931, the C chassis was introduced. This was essentially the same as the M, and even carried an M prefix to the chassis number. With the C chassis, the chassis tube was fitted with a center bearing and a basic but effective universal joint halfway along its length. This went a long way to removing propshaft vibration that plagued previous models, particularly when used in competition.

Later the same year, the Aero and Super Sports Aero were both in production as separate models, but with a common engine, the new sixty-degree JAP. The Aero was offered in either a two- or three-speed gearbox form, while the Super Sports Aero was only offered in three-speed gearbox form. Few two-speed Morgans were made in 1932, and the last one was supplied in 1933.

Prospects

The Aero, Aero Family and Super Sports Aero models must be regarded as ranking as second only to the Super Sports three-speed model in the popularity stakes as far as three-wheeler Morgans are concerned. The few that do come onto the market fetch high prices and are worthwhile investments.

The unique Morgan sliding pillar front suspension, the front wheel brakes and speedometer drive.

Super Sports Aero 1930 two-speed	
Engine	Overhead-valve, JAP LTOWC 10/40 hp, bore 85.7 mm, stroke 95 mm, high compression and specially tuned
Ignition	Magneto
Carburetor	Two-float sports motorcycle type
Lubrication	Mechanical with sight-feed
Transmission	Cone clutch
Suspension	Front: independent vertical helical springs with shock absorbers; rear: underslung quarter-elliptics
Wheels	19x3 in. wire
Tires	Fort Dunlop
Dimensions	Overall length 123 in., overall width 57 in.
Bodywork	"Special throughout. It is very well streamlined, the tail being hinged so that it can be lifted to gain access to the back wheel. The petrol tank is detachable and is fitted in front. The seats are slightly staggered. A pair of small windscreens are fitted, and the front wheels are covered by round cycle type fixed mudguards. The body and chassis can be painted any colour to choice."
Lamps	Electric set, 8 in. headlights with dimmers
Price	£128.10 including hood

This 1927 Aero is a permanent exhibit at the National Motor Museum, Beaulieu. In the dashboard layout, note the large electric horn push, which by this time was fitted as standard. The M-shaped footplate aided the less agile in getting into the car.

When the 1928 models were announced, a new model was included: the Super Sports Aero. The width of the bodywork was increased by 2½ inches and the rear wheel was entirely enclosed above the axle. Rounded at the back, the new Aero soon became known as the beetle-back. *D. Rushton and John H. Sheally II*

Super Sports 1932-39

The Super Sports Aero was introduced in the fall of 1927 for the 1928 season. The Aero and the Super Sports Aero models were produced side by side and with a choice of engines. This choice continued until the 1931 models were announced, and from then on the Aero model could be obtained with two distinct types of bodywork. The original style that was fitted with the B series chassis continued unchanged, but if supplied with the new M chassis, the Aero model also had a V-screen, and cycle-type mudguards—as did the Family Aero model.

In 1931 with the introduction of the three-speed gearbox, the Aero was offered with a two- or three-speed gearbox, but the Super Sports was only offered with a three-speed gearbox, and at the same time the V-screen was adopted as standard for the model. Initially, all models with the new three-speed gearbox were fitted with the new type JAP engine with a detachable handle front start. The new engine, whether air cooled or water cooled, side valve or overhead valve, had capacity of 1096 cc (85.7 mm x 95 mm). With the exception of the cylinders and valve gear, the several types were identical in design. All had dry-sump lubrication and were fitted with a Duplex Pilgrim oil pump. A one-gallon oil tank was mounted under the hood behind the engine, and oil was forced from this into the engine by one side of the double pump. The other half drained the surplus oil from a small sump and returned it to the oil tank. In this way, oil flowed continuously through the engine.

The Super Sports was fitted with the LTOWZ JAP sixty-degree overhead-valve water-cooled specially tuned version of the engine. The normal compression ratio was 6.9:1, but with the LTOWZ engine it was 7.5:1. This could be reduced by fitting compression shim plates. Modern owners of Super Sports fitted with this engine should remember that 7.5:1 was high even for a new engine running on the low octane fuel of the day. The more the cylinders are bored out or sleeved, the more the risk of serious damage is increased if the high compression

ratio is kept, as the engine has a distinct habit of deciding to break just below the water jacket and to distribute pieces over a wide area.

The width of the bodywork on the Super Sports was increased slightly, and the bonnet side louvers were replaced by a single D cutout. The plain cycle-type close-up front mudguards were replaced with the center-ribbed design but still retained the inner valance. The mudguard supporting stays remained the same as on other models, with a pin running through the sliding axle pivot tubes. This in turn was bent over to provide a flexible mounting, over the nineteen-inch non-detachable wheels.

In keeping with the Morgan tradition, these wings were not fitted with sidelights—and never were throughout the production of the model. The headlamps, which were mounted on top of vertical pillars that came off the top of the chassis crosstubes, were fitted with double filament bulbs. The main beam gave adequate light, but the dip position was little more than a parking light.

The cockpit was fitted with staggered seats, with the passenger slightly back, to enable the driver to have more elbowroom. The seats had the usual Morgan separate, single-back squab, covered in Rexine fabric in eight vertical pleats. The seat squabs were oblong cushions that were plain except for piping around the top edge. The sides of the cockpit and the dash were also covered in the same material. The foot wells were fitted with coconut mats.

The dash had an oval panel in the center in which were mounted the ignition and lighting switches, ignition warning light, ammeter, Cooper-Stewart needle-type speedometer and large horn button that the driver easily reached by extending the fingers of the left hand while the hand remained on the steering wheel. The horn was a six-volt Lucas Alette, usually fitted with a chromium-plated rim, which was mounted on the offside top chassis tube hanging downwards. The starter switch was mounted on the floor. For the traditionalists, a magneto version of the sixty-degree JAP was offered.

Originally pricing the Super Sports at £150, Morgan offered it for £5 less in 1931.

The cars were supplied in various color combinations, including wheels and the chassis.

A few minor changes were made during 1932, but all were only a prelude to the major changes announced in October of that year. The spring and sliding axle tubes were replaced with solid pivot pins, which were long enough to act for both the headlight mounting and mudguard stays. The problems of the gearbox's dripping oil and the complicated topping-up were removed by fitting leather oil seals and a proper filler cap in the top of the gearbox. In addition, the dynamo drive was changed from fiber wheel to a compressed fabric gear wheel. The distributor was updated by fitting a "Completely Water Proof" one.

The "New-Look Three-speed Super Sports" model was announced in October 1932 just before the Olympia Show and is therefore classed as a 1933 model. First, the factory attempted to introduce a one-chassis-for-all-models policy; this would not only be cheaper in the long run, but also would improve output. To this end, the chassis of the Super Sports was raised approximately one-half inch. This was achieved in two ways. First, Morgan reduced the bends in the front crosstubes. Second, the firm introduced eighteen-inch Dunlop Magna wheels. These wheels were not only detachable, but also interchangeable. This in turn meant that a spare wheel had to be provided, and this created quite a problem for the factory, as to where to mount the spare. After all, it had never had to face this problem before. The first solution was to mount the spare at an angle of almost forty-five degrees right on the point of the beetle-back top panel. This strange and rather laughable fixing created enormous drag and seriously re-

The Morgan works body erecting shop. In the left foreground is an almost completed Super Sports Aero. The filler cap in the passenger compartment shows that it was fitted with a rear-mounted oil tank. In the right foreground is an Aero model that was being fitted with the mottled dashboard, introduced in 1929. On the left, halfway down the shop is an example of the Delivery van with the rear sloping roof. *Morgan Motor Company*

STILL MORE WORLD'S RECORDS

RECORDS BROKEN BY MRS. G. M. STEWART DRIVING MR. W. D. HAWKES'S MORGAN

Sept. 12th, 1100 c.c.

50 Kilometres	-	-	-	103·43 m.p.h.
50 Miles	-	-	-	102·64 ,,
100 Kilometres	-	-	-	102·48 ,,

August 30th, 750 c.c.

5 Kilometres - - 100.64 m.p.h.

August 24th.

1100 c.c. Kilo (Flying Start) 115·6 m.p.h.	1100 c.c. Mile (Standing Start) 80·9 m.p.i.
,, Mile ,, ,, 114·8 ,,	750 c.c. Kilo (Flying Start) 99·1 ,,
,, Kilo (Standing Start) 70·4 ,,	,, Mile ,, ,, 98·1 ,,

(Subject to confirmation.)

The Morgan Runabout

LIST POST FREE FROM
MORGAN MOTOR CO., LTD.,
Malvern Link,
WORCESTERSHIRE.

The introduction of the 18 inch Dunlop Magna wheels on the 1933 Super Sports model created a problem for Morgan. Not only were the wheels detachable, but they were also interchangeable. This created the need for a spare—but where to mount it? The first and short-lived solution was to select a rather strange location. Soon, the spare was moved to lay on top of the panel behind the seats. *D. Rushton*

39

duced acceleration and top-speed figures. It received various names from the motoring public, none of which are printable. This type of mounting did not last long, and by December the spare wheel was mounted in a horizontal position on top of the tail.

Other alterations were also made, the most important of which was the introduction of a Borg & Beck single dry plate clutch instead of the leather cone clutch that had been fitted in various forms since the marque's conception. The new clutch was operated by the clutch pedal moving three toggle levers through a carbon ring. These levers withdrew a metal plate that was normally held in position against a light metal disc carrying a friction ring on each side; it was basically the same setup as the modern type of the same make, but had fewer splines on the propshaft and a solid center clutch plate. This was changed to a flexible center for the 1935 models.

At the same time, Morgan modified the steering arm on the off-side front wheel and lessened the angle of the sliding axles. In addition, it increased considerably the diameter of the mudguard stays, which were tubular and ran right up through the bearing for the sliding axle. It was claimed that this produced rather less camber and much lighter steering.

Body modifications were few but included a slight increase in the width of the front

The spare wheel problem was finally solved in mid-1935 with the introduction of the modification to the rear of the Super Sports bodywork to create the barrel-back. This 1935 MX-4 is owned by my good friend, and one of America's leading Morganeers, John H. Sheally II. In 1980 John decided to make his own tribute to the seventieth anniversary of the Morgan Motor Company. He and Tim Hund drove this Super Sports 3,328 miles from Virginia Beach to Los Angeles in 11 days—not, of course, without some mishaps. But he more than proved that a Morgan three-wheeler could still be used on US roads, even in modern traffic conditions. Did I hear someone say that magic word "gumball"? *John H. Sheally II*

The spare wheel remained mounted on top of the tail until 1935. But the exhaust pipes were lowered by about six inches due to burnt coat elbows. *D. Rushton*

end, so that there was an increase in foot-room. Also announced was an optional stain-less-steel radiator shell, but few, if any other than those for the show cars, were ever produced.

Last, chromium-plated exhaust pipes were lifted and carried back along the body waist-line, with the silencers starting in line with the back of the seats. Over the years, these were to cause many singed coat sleeves and in a few cases quite serious burns. For the 1935 models, the factory lowered the ex-haust pipes about six inches.

There were really only two design changes for the 1934 Super Sports. The cutouts on the bonnet side were extended to two D shapes as opposed to one, the second or rear one being more elongated than the first. In addition, all barrel-back models were fitted with a winged M mascot, rather on the lines of the Bentley flying B. The stork mascot that had been fitted for so many years to all Morgan models was still available as an extra for other models.

When the 1935 models were announced, the factory had lowered the exhaust pipes and made the most important change at the tail. The bodywork was altered to become barrel-shaped, similar to that of the F4 model. Instead of sloping away, it retained a

A close-up of John H. Sheally's 1935 Super Sports with Matchless MX-4 engine. It is a pity about the non-original headlamps, but he had to fit them to see his way across the United States in 1980. *John H. Sheally II*

more circular section right to the end. The spare wheel was mounted into a recess in the back panel of the tail. The hub and spokes, but not the tire or the wheel rim, were covered by a polished aluminum disc cover. This disc carried the number plate as well as the combined tail and number plate illumination lamp. On the top of the tail in the space previously used for the spare wheel mounting, a simple but effective luggage rack, consisting of three aluminum strips that ran lengthways, was mounted on two wooden bearers fixed across the tail. (Later the aluminum strips were replaced by a chromium-plated version.) The new design raised the following comment from the motor writer Ixion: "see the Super Sports Special, its tail end looks rather like a worms view of a beer bottle."

Two variations of the Super Sports were exhibited at the Olympia Show in 1935. The first was the original beetle-back model, powered by the sixty-degree JAP engine. The second was the new barrel-back model that had a new competition overhead-valve water-cooled 40 bhp Matchless MX4 engine, which was fitted with forked connecting rods in place of the side-by-side ones used in the MX and MX2 engines. The beetle-back model was slowly phased out, and with it the JAP LTOWZ engine, and was no longer included in the catalog by June 1935.

After the introduction of the four-wheeler in 1936, production of the three-wheelers continued alongside them, but the factory made few changes to the design. From 1936, the Super Sports was offered with a choice of either the Matchless MX2 or MX4 engine, water or air cooled. By mid-1939, the MX2 had been phased out. The only other modification worth mentioning is the introduction of Girling brakes in the 1938 models.

The dashboard of the 1935 MX-4 Super Sports. Note the St. Christopher medal mounted on the dashboard on the left-hand side. This replaced the flying stork mascot. The halved steering wheel is not original and was done to make the trip across the United States easier. *John H. Sheally II*

Prospects

When you speak of a Morgan three-wheeler, nearly everyone instantly visualizes a Super Sports. It is certainly the most popular model on the market, and a large number of them survive. Although it is a desirable model to purchase, the buyer must be prepared to invest a large bag of gold to acquire one in good condition.

Here a word of warning must be given to any prospective buyer of a Super Sports. Certain more unscrupulous persons, particularly in the past, have fitted the larger and longer Super Sports barrel-back tail to the later Sports model and then have attempted to, or managed to, pass the result off as the more popular and more expensive Super Sports when selling. The novice could easily be fooled, but to the expert, the deception is obvious. The 1932-39 Sports model has a far more upright bonnet, and the oil and petrol filler caps are much closer together on the Sports model. In addition, the beading around the cockpit is turned up instead of under, and there is no projection over the passenger side. However, sometimes the unscrupulous seller fitted the upswept exhaust pipes, and the deception was complete. Possibly, the original deception was practiced years ago, and the car has changed hands several times without its being noticed. All this tends to illustrate the necessity of employing a recognized expert to inspect the car of your dreams, no matter what the model, before you part with your hard-earned bag of gold. *Caveat emptor.*

This MX-2 engined Super Sports was the competition car used by the father and son combination, George and Jim Goodall, both of whom became directors of the Morgan Motor Company in turn. They were successful in competitions in both three- and four-wheeler Morgans in the 1930s.

Super Sports 1939 three-speed

Engine	Overhead-valve, Matchless 50 degree V-twin, bore and stroke 85.5 mm, 990 cc, detachable cylinder heads, Lo-ex pistons, forked connecting rods, roller-bearing big ends, fully floating gudgeon pins, enclosed rockers with positive lubrication
Ignition	Coil
Carburetor	Amal motorcycle type
Lubrication	Dry sump, one-gal oil tank
Gearbox	Morgan three-speed gearbox
Transmission	Single dry plate clutch with Borg & Beck flexible center
Suspension	Front: independent vertical enclosed helical springs with shock absorbers, rear: underslung steel quarter-elliptic springs
Brakes	Internal expanding
Wheels	18x3 in., Dunlop Magna, quickly detachable and interchangeable, spare wheel on rear panel removable to give access to rear forks
Tires	Dunlop
Dimensions	Overall length 124 in., overall width 59 in., wheelbase 87 in., track 50 in.
Bodywork	Sheet metal and wood, coachbuilt, easily removable from chassis, streamlined, Moseley Float-on-Air cushions, safety glass V-screen with Lucas pneumatic wiper, locker behind seat, folding hood with envelope, cycle-type wings, dummy radiator cap with streamlined M motive
Finish	Two-tone green: top of body dark green with lower panel wheels and chassis light green. Body and chassis black with choice of red, cream or green for wings and wheels, or body and chassis bright red with wheels and wings cream
Lamps	Electric set, 8 in. headlights with dimmers, taillamp
Electrics	Electric starter and horn
Price	£107 including hood, £3.10 for non-standard finish

Announced in early 1932, this Sports model was introduced as a replacement for the Aero model, and this could explain why so few three-speed Aeros were made. The Sports model could be ordered with one or two doors—or even no doors if you were energetic enough to step over the side of the bodywork. A feature retained for the whole of its production was a luggage locker behind the seats, which was large enough to accommodate two suitcases. The seats were upholstered with Dunlop Latex cushions and measured thirty-four inches wide overall and seventeen inches from front to back. The seat squab height was twenty inches. The car was also supplied with a hood as standard. The new single dry plate clutch received great praise from the motoring press as did the new design of ignition distributor. The bodywork had an upswept tail similar to the Family model of the same year.

In 1933, the body lines were improved with a squared-off tail panel and a spare wheel. This became the narrow barrel-back shape that did not overlap the tire of the spare wheel. The spare wheel was mounted on, rather than slightly in, the end panel. Originally, the factory supplied the following engine options: the JAP overhead-valve water-cooled LTOWZ or the side-valve LTWZ engine. By 1933, the Matchless MX engine was added to the list, and the Matchless MX2 in 1934. By 1935, the MX and the MX2 were the only options and were to remain so until 1937. Towards the end of that year, the MX4 was also added to the list. By 1939, the Sports model was only available with the Matchless MX2, and the model ceased with the outbreak of the war.

During the whole of its production run, the Sports model was offered with either a flat or V-screen, although few were fitted with the former. In addition, Morgan supplied a few cars to special order with upswept exhaust pipes like the Super Sports model.

Prospects

Assuming that you find an original example of the Sports model, then it is a worth-

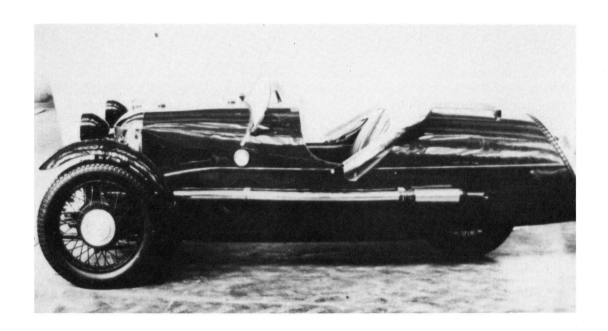

These two photographs illustrate the main differences between the Super Sports and the Sports models. The Super Sports petrol and oil filler caps are wide apart, and the spare wheel is set into the rear panel. In contrast with the Super Sports, on the Sports model the filler caps are much closer together, and the spare wheel is mounted on rather than in the rear panel. *D. Rushton*

while model to purchase and could turn out to be a good investment.

Sports 1932 and 1937 three-speed	
Engine	1932: JAP overhead-valve, bore 85.7 mm and stroke 95 mm, 1096 cc, water-cooled 1937: Overhead-valve, Matchless V-twin, bore and stroke 85.5 mm, 990 cc, air-cooled, detachable cylinder heads, enclosed rockers with positive lubrication
Ignition	Coil
Carburetor	Amal motorcycle type
Lubrication	1937: Dry sump, one-gal oil tank
Gearbox	Morgan three-speed gearbox
Transmission	Single dry plate clutch with Borg & Beck (1937: flexible center)
Suspension	Front: independent vertical enclosed helical springs with shock absorbers, rear: underslung steel quarter-elliptic spring
Brakes	Internal expanding
Wheels	1932: 19x3 in., not interchangeable 1937: 18x3 in., wire, Dunlop Magna, quickly detachable and interchangeable, spare wheel on rear panel removable for access to rear forks
Tires	Dunlop
Dimensions	1932: Overall length 130 in., overall width 57 in., wheelbase 84 in., track 48 in. 1937: Overall length 126 in., overall width 59 in., wheelbase 87 in., track 50 in.
Bodywork	Sheet metal and wood, coachbuilt, easily removable from chassis, streamlined 1932: Dunlop Latex cushions 1937: Moseley Float-on-Air cushions, safety glass V-screen, Lucas pneumatic wiper, locker behind seat, folding hood with envelope, cycle-type wings, dummy radiator cap with streamlined M motive
Finish	Blue and chrome standard finish, black and red with choice of green or cream wheels, usual parts chromium-plated
Lamps	Electric set 1932: headlamps main beam with pilot bulbs and taillamp 1937: 8 in. headlights with dimmers and taillamps
Electrics	Electric starter and horn
Price	1932: £120 overhead-valve, £110 side-valve 1937: £107 including hood and tools, £3.10 for non-standard finish

Ford-engined models 1933-52 ★★★

At some time in 1930, the Morgan factory started experimenting to produce a completely new design for its three-wheeler range. This model would be powered by a four-cylinder inline water-cooled engine. The engine favored was the Coventry Climax, and the prototypes included various sizes of this make as well as other manufacturers' engines.

In August 1932, the first all-British Ford was introduced and was named the Y model. The Y was powered by a 933 cc inline four-cylinder water-cooled side-valve engine, especially designed for the new Ford model by Laurence Sheldric, Ford's chief engineer. Coincidentally, the model Y was one of the last Ford models that Henry Ford was personally involved in.

In November 1933 at the Olympia Show, according to the motoring press, Morgan sprung an "Eleventh Hour Surprise": a Morgan with four cylinders. However, reporters were honest enough in the description to admit that "they had been privileged to see at various times experimental four-cylinder Morgan three-wheelers. Naturally it has not been permissible to publish anything concerning these machines until such time as the Morgan company completed its experiments, and was in a position to put the model into production."

The new model was named the F four-seater Morgan and is what we know today as the F4. Just as with the introduction of the three-speeders, the die-hard Morgan devotees just could not believe it. Gone was their beloved V-twin, and according to most, the model was a "car" yet with a wheel missing (although, of course, the V-twin was still available in other models). Just exactly how H.F.S. managed to acquire, test and negotiate the purchase of a regular supply of these Ford Y engines in such a short time is uncertain, but it all must once again point to his business acumen.

The Ford engine was more powerful than the Coventry Climax engine and was also cheaper. The engine was similar to that used in the 8 hp Ford Model Y, but was fitted with an aluminum alloy cylinder head, known as a Silver Top. This made it possible to have a higher compression ratio, and therefore greater power, making it capable of 70 mph while carrying four people. The petrol consumption figures were also good and ranged from 36 to 40 mpg according to use. All these were important factors to be taken into consideration when introducing a new model at a time when the £100 four-wheeled mass-produced cars had all but killed off the three-wheeler opposition.

Not only was the F four-seater model the first production Morgan fitted with a four-cylinder inline engine, but it also had other innovations. It was the first Morgan to be fitted with the now familiar Z section chassis, which is still basically the same design that is used in today's production Morgans. This new chassis design retained the tubular backbone through which the propeller shaft ran. The sides were made in a Z section from pressed steel. These were joined by two cross-members of channel section at the rear; on these the fixed end of the rear springs was bolted as well as the gearbox. Another piece of the Z section pressed steel was used as a cross-member and was welded to the side-members just behind the engine. At the front, the chassis sides are connected by an X-shaped steel pressing. To this, the front axle tubes were connected top and bottom, plus the radius arms between the axle and the chassis sides. The Z section was arranged so that the lower flanges faced inward, and the top therefore faced outward. This made convenient fixing points for the floorboards and the body sides.

Another change from all the V-twin models was that the clutch and brake foot pedals were mounted on a short cross-shaft, and for the first time the foot brake operated on all three wheels, while the handbrake operated on the rear wheel only. From one end of the cross-shaft, a Bowden cable passed to the rear brake. From the other end of the cross-shaft, a rod sloped upward toward the front axle and on the end of this rod was a small pulley wheel held in a yoke. A bracket was fitted on the front axle with two more

A Morgan with four cylinders was the surprise of the 1933 Motor Cycle Show at Olympia. Named the F four-seater Morgan, it soon became known as the F4. Powered by a Ford Y engine, it was a complete departure from the Morgan traditional V-twin engines. *D. Rushton*

For the 1936 season, Morgan announced an addition to the F range, the F four-cylinder, two-seater model, which we now refer to as the F2. It was offered with a choice of an 8 hp or 10 hp Ford engine. *D. Rushton*

pulleys mounted side by side in it. A single Bowden cable passed from one front brake, around one of the axle pulleys, around the brake rod pulley and then around the second front axle pulley to the front brake on the opposite side. In this simple manner, complete compensation of the system was obtained.

The steering layout was also altered with the track rod and the drag link positioned in front of the axle, but the reduction box on the steering column was retained. Both these features were incorporated into the original design of the four-wheeler when it was introduced in 1936, but the latter was dispensed with in the first year of production.

Other added luxuries were a foot-pedal-operated throttle plus the then conventional lever on the steering wheel. Both were connected to the throttle on the engine, and therefore the acceleration could be controlled from either—the best of both worlds, and possibly the forerunner of cruise control!

The first production F4 left the factory on April 25, 1934. Its chassis number was FD1, and it was fitted with Ford engine number Y38054.

Initially, the model was fitted with close wheel following cycle-type front fenders, which fitted close to and followed the arch of the wheel rim, but before the next Olympia show they had been changed to the long flowing type. The standard color scheme was Saxe Blue, black fenders and cream wheels. By this time, the rear end had also been modified slightly to provide a better mounting of the spare wheel, so that it fitted further into the recess in the tail, making a smoother line. All post-World War Two works-produced models were fitted with the flowing fenders. After the last twenty left the factory in 1952, a few were assembled by enthusiasts who bought a complete set of parts from the factory.

The 1935 Motor Cycle Show at Olympia was to see the addition of another model in the Morgan Ford-engined range for the 1936 season. Although given various names by the public, such as "A new Super Sports" or "A new Sports Model," the official name

allocated to it by the factory was the "F Four-cylinder, Two-seater model," which we now refer to as the F2. The prototype had been extensively tested in M.C.C. Trials by George Goodall; its registration number was BGO 8.

From the time of its announcement, the new model was offered with or without a door and with a choice of either an 8 hp or 10 hp 1172 cc engine. The more powerful engine that was from the prewar C Ford 10

Ford-engined 1934 four-seater	
Engine	Ford
Type	Four cylinders inline, water-cooled
Bore and stroke	56.6 mm x 92.5 mm
Displacement	933 cc
Valve	Side, enclosed
Compression	7:1, fitted with Silver Top alloy head
Carburetor	Zenith down-draft
Ignition	Lucas coil, with automatic advance and retard, six-volt dynamo
Chassis	Deep Z section steel pressings, with tubular backbone enclosing propeller shaft
Clutch	Single dry plate, connected to gearbox by short shaft enclosed in tube
Gearbox	Three-speed
Final drive	Worm driven cross-shaft and final ¾ in. chain to rear wheel
Suspension	Front: independent enclosed coil springs. Rear: straight laminated leaf spring
Brakes	Foot pedal operating on all three wheels, hand lever on rear only, 7 in. front and 8 in. rear drums
Wheels	18x3 in., Dunlop Magna, detachable and all interchangeable
Tires	26x4 in., Dunlop
Dimensions	Wheelbase 99 in., track 50 in., overall width 59 in., overall length 138 in., ground clearance 6½ in.
Weight	893 lb.
Controls	Spring steering wheel with throttle-setting lever and light dipping switch; accelerator, clutch and brake pedals; gear lever in gate, brake lever with ratchet for parking. On dashboard: electric starter switch, horn button, ammeter, trip speedometer, ignition switch, and tell-tale lighting switch, instrument lamp, and carburetor starting control. Windscreen wiper motor on driver's side
Windscreen	Fixed on F4, fold flat on F2 as from 1936
Finish	Painted wheels; chromium-plated lamps, radiator, windscreen frame and hubcaps
Price	£120

or the postwar E93A Ford series proved to be almost as powerful as the Matchless MX4 engine in the Super Sports, and as it cost only £7 more, many customers considered the extra expense worthwhile. Although giving only an extra 4 mph on the top speed, the acceleration rate was a considerable improvement on the 8 hp engine. The model was supplied in a variety of color combinations at extra cost, but the most impressive was always held to be the two-tone cream and scarlet. Prices in 1937 for the 8 hp versions were £115.10 for the F4 and £120.15 for the F2.

When Morgan announced the 1938 models, yet another new model appeared in the Ford-engined range. Officially named the F Super Sports by the factory, it is now known as the F Super. This model combined the front half of the F2 bodywork with the rear end of the V-twin Super Sports. From the front, the model could be identified by the additional line of louvers down the tops of both halves of the hood and the cycle-type front fenders. Completing the sporting image was a fold-down windscreen.

Prospects

In an interview with the motoring press in 1950, H.F.S. said of the F models, "This was the best all-round three-wheeler we have turned out, and with slight modifications, it is in production today." This view was not altogether shared by buyers, and the model does not enjoy as much popularity as might be thought. It does of course have its devotees, one of whom (at the time of writing) has owned a 1937 F4 since he bought it new in that year. He is seventy-eight-year-old Gerald Carr.

Strangely, in spite of its good performance and easily obtained engine parts, the F models have never been popular with the present-day buying public. From the head-on view one can mistake it for a four-wheeler, and maybe this is the reason for its lack of popularity. However, without doubt I recommend it as a model that is going to increase in value in the next few years.

In 1915, H.F.S. Morgan invented a system whereby a hood could be erected while the car was in motion. Here the principle is being demonstrated on an F4 40 years later. *D. Rushton*

At the 1937 Motor Cycle Show, Morgan announced yet another new model to its F range, named the F Super Sports, but soon referred to as the F Super. This model can be identified by the additional louvers down the tops of both halves of the bonnet, motorcycle fenders and fold-down windscreen. *D. Rushton*

Chapter 2

Morgan 4-4 and 4/4

In 1931, the Morris Motor Company introduced the first £100 motorcar. Morris was closely followed by two other mass producers, although it was rumored that both these companies sold at below cost to stay in competition. The availability of a cheap "proper" motorcar, effectively put an end to the sales of cyclecars, and particularly three-wheelers.

As Britain recovered from the Depression, the major manufacturers took a large proportion of the lower end of the market, with such models as the Austin 7, Ford 8, Hillman Minx and Morris 8. Although mass-produced, these cars offered four-wheel motoring, with comfort, economy and saloon car weather protection, and they cost in most cases only £3 or £5 more in taxation a year than three-wheelers.

In an attempt to stem the drift away from three-wheelers by the public, the major manufacturers of these cyclecars increased the number of models available. By December 1932, BSA offered six versions of its front-wheel drive car, and Coventry-Victor six also, while Morgan offered five different models.

In a further attempt to promote the virtues of the three-wheeler, the motoring press increased its coverage of three-wheeler related topics. *The Lightcar and Cyclecar* magazine even introduced a regular contribution entitled "On Three Wheels," from a journalist with the pen-name Triangle. All this was to no avail, and the three-wheeler's share of the market steadily declined. At the

Motor Show at Olympia in 1935, five manufacturers exhibited their cars, as compared to eleven in 1929. In his budget on April 28, 1936, Neville Chamberlain, the chancellor of the exchequer, announced that the government intended to abolish road fund tax on all motor vehicles in 1937. This effectively finished off light cars and cyclecars with both three and four wheels. At the motorcycle show in October 1936, only the Morgan Motor Company exhibited a three-wheeler.

By shrewd thinking and application of his business acumen, H.F.S. Morgan averted possible closure by the development and introduction of the Morgan four-wheeler. Announced in the motoring press on December 26, 1935, it was to prove to be the savior of the company. To the Morgan three-wheeler stalwarts, the extra wheel was sacrilege. However, they had their cars, and their loyalty was not going to pay the bills, increase wages or keep the jam on the bread.

It was never H.F.S. Morgan's intention to attempt to capture the luxury sports car market. For twenty-six years, he had produced the everyman's sports car with outstanding performance, but without any of the embellishment that always rocketed the price. After all, Brough Superior, Bugatti, Lagonda, Hotchkiss, Delage, Talbot, Lancia and many others were all quite happily committing economic suicide in their attempts to capture and hold the market for limited, expensive, large-engined, heavily taxed, open sports cars or the similar sports saloons. In contrast, H.F.S. had always basically aimed at and captured the market made up of the motoring public who longed to own a well-made, reliable, economical sports car. The average wage of the day was very low, so these ordinary people could not afford to buy a car that cost them five to ten years' wages. To buy a Morgan that offered nearly all the advantages of the expensive sports car, but cost them under a year's wages, and to buy a Morgan whose performance was vastly in excess in proportion to cost must have been the answer for an aspiring sports car owner.

For the new car to succeed it needed to prove itself in competition, however. This the Morgan four-wheeler did, performing well in both national and international events, such as M.C.C. Trials, road rallies,

racing and the Le Mans twenty-four-hour races. With the onset of World War Two, the Morgan factory was once again made over to the manufacture of military items for the war effort, but this time not even limited production of cars was allowed.

After hostilities ended, H.F.S. quickly established agents in North America and France, so that he could receive an allocation of steel in order to get the factory back into full production as soon as possible. Government restrictions meant that sheet steel for use in the motor industry was available to those companies capable of exporting. These export markets—coupled with the introduction of Triumph TR4 engined Plus 4s and the Plus 4 Super Sports models as well as the major international competition successes they achieved, including the Le Mans twen-

The original prototype 4-4 was nothing more than a straightening of the three-wheeler F4 chassis and the fitting of a two-wheel rear axle. The rear wheels and the seat appear to have been added almost as an afterthought. The 4-4's

inheritance from the F4 is even more pronounced when we realize it was powered by the same Ford 8 hp engine. This car was photographed at Stanway, H.F.S. Morgan's home. *Morgan Motor Company*

ty-four-hour race—were to prove to be the saving of the company in the 1960s.

H.F.S. Morgan's death in June 1959 was a great loss to all who had any connections with the Morgan Motor Company. He was succeeded by his son P.H.G. Morgan who is still the chairman and managing director of the company. There can be no doubt that Peter Morgan has inherited his father's business acumen. He has carefully steered the company through several crises, including a takeover bid by a major manufacturer in the mid-sixties.

At the same time, the marque has become *the* sports car to own. In spite of the world-wide recession in recent years, there is still a three- to five-year waiting list, depending on which model you have ordered. This in turn has increased the demand for secondhand examples, especially older models. Cars that ten years ago could be purchased for £500 now easily fetch five or six times that amount, if you can find them. At the same time, many specialist service companies have been formed to deal with the demand that such popularity brings.

4-4 flat-radiator models	
1936-51	
Drophead coupe	★★★★
Two- and four-seaters	★★★

The introduction of the four-wheeled Morgan in 1936 was born of necessity. The company experimented with the idea twice before, but for various reasons, had shelved it. By the end of 1934, a four-wheeler was a necessity for Morgan's survival.

Using the now famous Z section chassis and the Ford 8 hp 993 cc side-valve engine of the F three-wheeler, he produced a basic, testbed prototype. The vehicle was really nothing more than an F rolling chassis, including the windshield. From there, the chassis continued parallel with a two-wheeled standard rear axle fitted. Two bucket seats were bolted to the chassis, and the rear wheels had flat pieces of steel plate, slightly bent to follow the wheel line, mounted on outriggers acting as rear fend-

ers. This experimental car, assigned chassis number 1, was never registered for the road and was used on the company's trade plates.

The experiments proved that the sluggish Ford engine was not powerful enough for the job. H.F.S. then looked around for an alternative engine of comparable size and decided to experiment with a Coventry Climax engine. Thousands of these engines had been produced in various forms and had a good reputation for durability. Two more experimental cars were built, this time with full road-going bodywork, and underwent exhaustive road and track trials throughout 1935. In July of that year, a staff member of *The Light Car and Cyclecar* magazine was allowed to test-drive the car with designated chassis number 3 at the famous Brooklands racetrack. By this time, chassis number 2 was discarded, having served its purpose well. The test car was driven at speeds in excess of 70 mph, but the report was not published until Christmas 1935, when the model was officially announced. The first production car was not delivered until March 1936.

When announced, the model was assigned the name 4-4. This was chosen because the car had four wheels and four cylinders. This simple formula has been used for deciding model names for all four-wheeled Morgans since. (Immediately after the war, the works for some obscure reason changed the actual style of the name, changing it from the original 4-4 to 4/4. This style has been the norm ever since.) The flat-radiator 4-4s are often referred to today as Series Is, but they are strictly speaking 4-4s. Coincidence or not, the first production car was chassis number 4, and the first one to be exported was chassis number 44, which went to Stewart Sandford in Paris.

The 1122 cc version of the Coventry Climax engine, used from March 1936 to September 1939, was found to have far better performance than the Ford, this in spite of its complicated layout of overhead inlet and side exhaust valves, plus thermo-syphon cooling. This meant that it was far more in keeping with the sporting reputation that the marque had built up over the years. Pro-

Early 4-4s were fitted with a wire mesh radiator grille, which was standard until late 1938 when Morgan began to use the upright slatted grille. The wire mesh was still available as an option right up to World War Two. *Morgan Motor Company*

duced initially as a two-seat roadster, it quickly started to earn what was to become an illustrious competition record. By 1937, demand was comfortably outstripping the company's production capacity. This in turn led to the introduction of the four-seat tourer version, closely followed by the drop-head coupe.

The prototype of the 4-4 drophead coupe model was made in early 1938; the first production coupe was built in October 1938. It was really an experimental car, powered by the prototype Standard Special engine, which was later adopted by the company. Morgan had no experience making this style of body, so a rolling chassis two-seater was sent to the Avon Body Company at Ross-on-Wye. The resulting body was so attractive that H.F.S. immediately took the car for his own personal transport. Using this bodywork as a basis, the company designed their own even more attractive two-seater bodywork.

The twenty-six-inch-wide rear-hinged doors had no cutaway at the top; recesses cut in the inner panel of the doors provided elbowroom. The doors were fitted with detachable windows, which consisted of two panes that slid in either direction sideways in a metal frame, allowing front or rear ventilation. For more ventilation while the hood was erected, you opened flaps fitted to the side walls of the scuttle. Semaphore-type turn indicators were fitted immediately behind the doors. The hood opened in any of three positions: fully closed, fully open or rolled back and fastened immediately behind the occupants' heads in the coupe de ville position. Wider section sixteen-inch steel disc-type wheels, slatted radiator grille, leather upholstery, wood-capped interior, chromed body trim, twin upright spare wheels and optional two-tone paintwork made for an acceptable, albeit rather pedantic (because of the extra weight), version of the 4-4.

From March 1939, many were fitted with the smaller but more powerful 1098 cc Coventry Climax competition engine and from July 1939 with the 1267 cc Standard Special engine. These two alternatives won many

competition honors, both as works' and private entries.

Triumph was producing Coventry Climax engines under license for their Gloria Southern Cross models and also for the Crossley Regis. These engines were 1087 cc, and a competition version was also produced to uprate their cars for competition work. Coventry Climax wanted to add a similar competition engine to its range, but it was too small to produce them in large quantities. It was therefore arranged for Triumph to produce them under license. Triumph did not have the capacity or the manpower to produce a fully tuned competition engine so it compromised by producing some bolt-on accessories that improved the engine's performance even more.

The basic engine was still the inlet-over-exhaust-valve model already being supplied to Morgan. This engine was under-bored to 63.2 mm, giving a 1098 cc displacement, bringing the engine into the popular international under 1100 cc competition class. The engines were balanced throughout, including the flywheel, but did not have polished ports. Morgan fitted these engines as an option to standard chassis cars with normal bodywork, including drophead coupes, for those owners who wanted the extra performance: 56 bhp at 4500 rpm.

The bolt-on extras that improved the performance even more were supplied by Triumph only to order. These consisted of a four-branch internal and external tapering exhaust manifold that produced a venturi effect. This was fitted directly into a Burgess straight-through silencer.

Carburetion, either Solex or Zenith, had a larger than normal choke tube. The adding of these extras increased the power to 56–60 bhp at 4500 rpm. Any Morgan to be fitted with the complete competition engine had to have its bodywork altered to accommodate the exhaust manifold. This consisted of removing the normal swept front fenders and the running boards and then fitting cycle-type front fenders that were fixed and did not turn with the front wheels (unlike many British cars of the period). The nearside of the hood had to be altered as well.

By the beginning of 1938, Triumph was in serious financial difficulties, and H.F.S. could see that it would not be long before his supply of Coventry Climax engines would end. Triumph eventually went bankrupt in June 1939, and H.F.S. approached his old friend John Black, who was by then head of the Standard Motor Company, to see if he could supply a suitable engine. (John Black, a bright young man in 1909, had actually produced the patent drawings for the Morgan Runabout for H.F.S.) The Standard Motor Company was already producing sports car engines for Jaguars, although Standard's own cars were anything but sporting. John Black agreed to design and produce an overhead-valve version of his 1267 cc 10 hp side-valve engine. The result was an engine that produced more power than the 1122 cc Coventry Climax engine, and more importantly, the engine did not move the car into a higher taxation class (in those days the yearly road

In mid-1937, a special short chassis version of the 4-4 was built by the factory for sporting trials work. It offered more weight over the rear wheels. This car, now owned by Roger Comber, was Peter Morgan's personal trials car and was very successful.

tax was decided by a complicated formula based on an engine's horsepower).

The first experimental Standard Special 1267 cc engine was fitted to a first drophead coupe in about May 1938, with the second and third experimental engines being fitted in two works' trials cars, a two-seater and another drophead coupe, in December. Further trials were carried out in April 1939, and the first production car fitted with the new 1267 cc engine was sold in July 1939. In all, thirty-eight cars including the experimental cars were produced before World War Two commenced and the works was turned over to the production of parts for the war effort.

Postwar production was erratic, with orders far outstripping the number of cars that could actually be produced. When materials were made available, it was done so on the strict understanding that at least ninety percent of any company's production was exported. In fact, a few production cars were sent away to outside companies for paneling. These were companies who were allocated sheet metal but did not have the orders to use up their quotas. The remainder of each car, including the woodwork, had been

All 4-4s were fitted with black-faced instruments and a Brooklands steering wheel. The large push button in the center of the dash, below the speedometer, sounds the horn. *Morgan Motor Company*

constructed at the works. It was not until January 1948 that the factory managed to return to full production again.

Production of the Standard Special engine 4-4 ended in February 1951.

Prospects

The Coventry Climax-engined 4-4s strangely have not commended such a high price in the market as other contemporary marques of sports cars. The reasons for this are rather obscure, but over the last two or three years, prices have increased steadily. It could be that at long last buyers are turning to them because of their comparatively low prices and the lack of other marques on the market.

In terms of use, undoubtedly this model can hold its own in modern traffic conditions. Of all the models, the four-seater is perhaps the least desirable, but even this offers comparatively good performance. With all examples of this model, those fitted with the Moss gearbox have the edge on acceleration and top speed. The drophead coupes fitted with the Coventry Climax engine, and in particular the 1098 cc version,

This completely restored 1949 drophead coupe belongs to Bob Burrows of Ohio. The windows in the doors slide sideways. The 4-4 drophead coupe is now a sought after model and represents a good investment.

are much sought after, and those few examples known to survive rarely come on the market.

Few prewar examples of the 4-4 fitted with the Standard Special 1267 cc engine were produced, and comparatively, even fewer are known to survive. In spite of the better overall performance of the overhead-valve engine, the cars with them do not command such a high price as the Coventry Climax models. Without doubt, the drop-head coupe is the most sought after version of the 4-4, with the four-seater being the least popular and a model which will slowly rise in value.

4-4 flat-radiator	
Engine	Coventry Climax
Type	Four cylinders inline, water-cooled (thermo-syphon), cast-iron block and cylinder head
Bore and stroke	63 mm x 90 mm
Displacement	1122 cc
Valve	Overhead inlet and side exhaust
Brake horsepower	34 at 4500 rpm
Chassis	Z section steel pressings, under-slung, with inverted U-section cross-members
Clutch	Borg & Beck single dry plate, connected to gearbox by short shaft enclosed in tube
Gearbox	Meadows four-speed
Final drive	By open Hardy Spicer propeller shaft with needle-bearing universals to conventional back axle with spiral bevel gears in pressed steel banjo case
Front suspension	Independent with sliding stub axle assemblies on vertical pillars, upper enclosed and lower exposed coil springs with Newton telescopic shock absorbers
Rear suspension	Half-elliptic laminated springs, underslung, 40 in. between centers, Andre frictional shock absorbers
Brakes	Girling, 8 in. drum, rod and cable operation
Wheels	Pressed disc type with hubcaps, four-stud fitting
Tires	5x16 in., Dunlop, extra-low-pressure
Dimensions	Wheelbase 92 in., length 140 in., width 54 in., height 44 in. (49 in. with hood up), track 45 in.
Weight	Dry 1,232 lb., wet 1,512 lb.

4-4 Le Mans Special, Le Mans Replica and TT Replica	

Early in 1938, Miss Prudence Fawcett decided that she would like to compete in the Le Mans twenty-four-hour race. After long discussion with friends of the Fawcett family, namely Rivers Fletcher and Lancelot Prideaux-Brune who owned Winter Garden Garages, one of Morgan's main distributors, it was decided to approach several different British motor manufacturers to see if any would be willing to loan a car for this enterprise. At least three replied that they would. After discussion it was decided that the Morgan would offer the best chance of success because the 1098 cc Coventry Climax engine offered the best potential for tuning. A perfectly standard two-seater was collected from the works along with the set of bolt-on extras in March or April.

At this time, the 1098 cc engine had not as yet been fitted to a production car. One had been used in the 4-4 works car entered in the 1937 R.A.C. Tourist Trophy Race, held at Donington, the first time that the race had been held in England. The car was driven by H. Laird, who had earned a formidable reputation on the racetrack with his supercharged Morgan three-wheeler. The car did well until it broke a stub-axle in the eighty-fourth lap.

When the car loaned by Morgan arrived at Winter Garden Garages at Birmingham, it was completely stripped down and reconstructed so as to remove the maximum possible weight within safety limits, these having been decided after discussions with the Morgan works. This included the removal of the front fenders and running boards and their replacement with cycle-type fenders as previously described. The rear panel was removed from immediately below the luggage compartment lip where the tonneau cover was fitted. The nine-gallon fuel tank was replaced by a twenty-four-gallon tank constructed to fit the space above and behind the rear axle. Two racing quick-fill filler pipes and caps were placed through the tonneau cover where the hood and sidescreen storage compartment was normally located. The rear panel was replaced with a solid flat panel that followed the sweep of the fenders. Two spare wheels were mounted one on top of the other, on top of the panel and at the same angle; only one spare was carried in competition.

The engine was also completely stripped down and race-tuned by the garage's chief racing mechanic Dick Anthony, who was to be Miss Fawcett's co-driver in the race. In addition, seventeen-inch spoked disc wheels were fitted instead of the normal sixteen-inch. The gearbox and rear axle ratios were also increased. Chronometric instruments, including a tachometer, were fitted. The car was tested several times at the Brooklands racetrack before being driven on the road all the way to Le Mans. The entry received no works' support, other than the supplying of the car. The pits were manned by Winter Garden Garages owner, Lancelot Prideaux-Brune.

Amazingly, at two in the morning the Morgan was leading the whole field by a considerable margin. This position was maintained until mid-morning when the car started to overheat due to a leaking radiator, caused by vibration. Pit stops to take on fuel and water were strictly controlled, and the car had to drive carefully so as to last to the end of the race. The careful driving paid off, and the Morgan was one of only two British cars to finish. The final position was thirteenth overall and second in class, and the

In 1938, Miss Prudence Fawcett decided that she would like to compete in the Le Mans twenty-four-hour race. With the aid of family friends in the motor trade, she secured the loan of a 4-4 from the Morgan works for the race.

The race car was driven on the road all the way to Le Mans. It waited to be lifted by crane onto the cross channel ferry. Note the two spare wheels mounted on top of the sloping flat panel at the rear.

Morgan covered 1,372.98 miles at an average speed of 57.2 mph.

After the race, the car was eventually returned to the works and was then entered in the Tourist Trophy Race but failed to finish; again this was due to overheating caused by a leaking radiator. Before the 1939 Le Mans, the spare wheel had been lowered into a recess in the sloping tail. At the same time, H.F.S.'s personal trials car and one or two other works' competition cars were rebodied in the same style, but not necessarily fitted with the full competition engine and bolt-on extras. The simple act of lowering the spare wheel produced *three* distinct limited production models, although only one of them was ever officially announced.

The Morgan works as usual were not slow to capitalize on a competition success. They immediately produced a Le Mans Special, the works' name designation. This was the

Final checks are carried out before the practice for the race. Only one spare wheel was mounted, and the number plate was removed before the race.

first of the three models. These cars had a normal production body, from the scuttle back to and including the twin upright spare wheels. In front of the scuttle, the cars were fitted with cycle-type front fenders. They had the 1098 cc Coventry Climax engine with the four-branch exhaust manifold. In all, seven of these Specials were produced between June 1938 and September 1939, six two-seaters and one four-seater.

The second model was known as a TT Replica, although it was never officially designated or announced as a production model. It had the sloping rear panel with a single spare wheel mounted on top of it following the same sweep, cycle-type front fenders, full competition engine, nine-gallon fuel tank with twin filler caps in the sloping back panel immediately above the spare wheel and a normal cover over the luggage compartment. This was the same configuration as the 1937 Tourist Trophy race car as well as the 1938 Le Mans and Tourist Trophy race car. In all, four cars were made or converted to this body design.

The third model was the Le Mans Replica model, officially announced in February 1939 and which was to sell at £250. This model had the spare wheels mounted so that the bottom one was partly inserted in a recess cut in the rear sloping tail. The same modification was made to the 1939 Le Mans race car. The Le Mans Replica model was fitted with a full 1098 cc competition engine and cycle-type front fenders. The Le Mans back-up car was bored out to 1104 cc as was the actual race car. The storage compartment tonneau cover was replaced by a hinged metal lid that opened to a small trunk, with a removable floor to give access to the rear axle. The hinged lid followed the curve of the fenders and back panel from immediately behind the seats, giving a more streamlined appearance. A nine-gallon fuel tank and twin fillers were fitted as with the TT Replicas. The car used for press photographs for this announcement was the specially constructed Le Mans back-up car.

The decision to race again in the 1939 Le Mans was made because the car had qualified for the final of the Rudge-Whitworth Biennial Cup competition in the 1939 event.

On this occasion, the car was driven by Dick Anthony and another employee of Winter Garden Garages, Geoffrey White. This year, the works was to be officially involved in the event and prepared a back-up car that was identical in every detail to the actual race car. Charlie Curtis, Morgan's chief tester, who was in charge of the pits drove the back-up car to Le Mans, but this was not raced. Both cars were bored out to 1104 cc to move them up into the next class where it was thought they would stand more chance of winning. The strategy worked, and the car finished fifteenth overall, covering a distance of 1,548.62 miles at an average speed of 64.53 mph, and was the highest-placed British car in the Rudge-Whitworth Biennial Cup.

Immediately after the race, both cars returned to the works where they were checked over and retuned. The works had entered the Tourist Trophy Race again, but with the onset of war being inevitable, the works accepted an offer made for the actual race car, and it was sold as a secondhand vehicle to America and has not been traced since. Both cars were converted to a nine-gallon fuel tank for ordinary road use. Originally, Morgan intended to use the back-up car as a works' competition and road test car, but the war was declared, and the cars were placed in store along with two rolling chassis fitted with 1098 cc competition engines and two or three of the works' competition cars, including those of H.F.S. and Peter Morgan.

After the war, the two finished cars were overhauled and repainted, the back-up car yellow with black wings and the other all white. It again was the works' intention to use them as competition cars, but the back-up car was sold by mistake in 1946 (a director of the company even unsuccessfully attempted to buy it back a week after its sale). As a result of this, the other Le Mans Replica was also sold in 1946. The other two chassis were bodied and sold in 1947, one as a Le Mans Replica and the other as a normal two-seater 4-4 that was exported to France. Morgan recorded all three cars as Le Mans Replicas and allocated postwar chassis numbers to correspond with the sales dates.

After nearly twenty years of extensive research, I have at last been able to establish exactly how these special 4-4s were designated and the total production figures for each example. The final piece of the jigsaw appeared during the writing of this book, when the four-seater version of the Le Mans Specials was discovered in a garage complete with the original registration documents and so on. This, in conjunction with other known examples, photographic evidence from the private collection of Miss Prudence Fawcett and many hours of studying the factory records, enables me to establish the production details of these special models.

Seven Le Mans Specials were built. Six were fitted with twin upright spare wheels, but with 1098 cc engines, four-branch exhausts and cycle-type front fenders. In addition, one four-seater with the normal single upright spare wheel was produced to the same specifications.

Four TT Replicas were built, with the spare wheel mounted on top of the rear

Both drivers needed to become as familiar as possible with the course during practice, so Miss Fawcett and Dick Anthony traveled together for part of the time. The windscreen was folded flat, with the driver's Aero-screen visible. The large screen was removed for the actual race.

After its success in the Le Mans, the same Coventry Climax-engined car was entered in the Tourist Trophy race in Donington later in 1938. Here workers prepared the car for the race.

Morgan rebodied one or two of the works competition cars in the style of the Le Mans/TT car. The works' car CAB 652 competed in the 1938 Lands End Trail, with a standard two-seater body.

The works rebodied CAB 652 as a TT Replica.
The single spare wheel rested on rather than in
the sloping tail panel.

For the 1939 Le Mans race, the rear panel of the car was altered so that the spare wheel sat in rather than on the sloping rear panel. Only two sections of the tire tread pattern are visible above the panel. Geoffrey White and Dick Anthony, who shared the driving, relaxed with a cigarette after finishing fifteenth place overall.

Seven Le Mans Specials were built by the works. Six received normal bodies, except for cycle-type front fenders. The seventh had a normal body except for the rear panel, which sloped with the spare wheel resting on top of the panel, similar to the actual Le Mans and TT car tail. The four-branch exhaust must have been modified to clear the front fender, but the car is listed in the works records as a Le Mans Special. All were fitted with 1098 cc Coventry Climax competition engines, complete with four-branch exhausts. Here the works car competes in the 1938 RAC Rally, crewed by father and son G. H. and W. A. Goodall, who were class winners in 1937, 1938 and 1939.

A Le Mans Special, at the start of the Morgan 4/4
Club's first road rally in 1951, was owned and
driven by Bill Allerton who won the event.

One of the Le Mans Specials was a four-seater, with a standard body (they all only had one spare wheel) but was fitted with cycle-type front fenders. This car was discovered in 1988, having been laid up in 1939 when war was declared, and although partially stripped, it was complete. The odometer had only 8,500 miles recorded.

Morgan made only three Le Mans Replicas. All
were constructed before the war, but were not
sold until 1946 and 1947. This is the author's car,
with an inserted spare wheel and metal boot lid.

panel, 1098 cc engine, four-branch exhaust and cycle-type front fenders. This number includes the actual Tourist Trophy race car and those converted to this specification.

Three Le Mans Replicas were built, with sloping rear with insert spare wheel. This number includes the actual race back-up car.

One or two works' trials cars were rebodied in the Le Mans Replica style but were never production examples of that model.

In addition to these special models, the factory fitted the 1098 cc engine to standard production models, including both the four-seater and the drophead coupe. It was offered as an alternative option to the normal 1122 cc engine at a slightly increased price but was not supplied with the bolt-on extras as mentioned. The works would specially tune this engine, if requested.

Prospects

The whereabouts of some of these cars is not known. As illustrated by the discovery of the four-seater Le Mans Special, keep your eyes open and you may find one of the missing ones in the back of a barn or a garage somewhere. However, do not waste your time trying to locate the 1939 Le Mans back-up car because it has had a warm garage to my knowledge for the past thirty-five years, and the owner has no intention of parting with it.

The Le Mans and TT Replica models are fast through the gears and at top speed, mainly due to the reduced weight and streamlined body style. Their performance is much more in keeping with that expected from a sports car. Next comes the Le Mans Special, but to a lesser degree due to the standard rear end of the body. Then, of course, come the specially tuned examples of the 1098 cc engines. From this it must not be construed that the two-seater is slow and not sought after. Quite the contrary, they did and still do perform well in competition. All examples of this model can only increase in value over the years.

Another of the Le Mans Replicas, originally owned by Aileen Jarvis, competed in an early 4/4 Club driving test. The two spare wheels are mounted on top of one another.

This series of photographs illustrate all the special items peculiar to the Le Mans Replica model. Note the four-branch exhaust, cycle-type front fenders, inserted spare wheel, tachometer and so on. The klaxon fitted is not original.

From the initial concept of a four-wheeled version of the Morgan, the company had from time to time experimented with various Ford engines, the most popular being the 10 hp version. This size engine, although fulfilling H.F.S. Morgan's desire to keep the capacity down just in case the government reintroduced the horsepower-rated taxation system, was not robust enough, nor did it produce power enough to be a viable proposition for a sports car.

By 1955, it was becoming increasingly obvious to the Morgan Motor Company that a large gap existed in the market for a low-priced production sports car. It so happened that at this time Ford had just redesigned its 10 hp engine, making it stronger and more powerful than ever before, without altering the outside dimensions.

Enquiries revealed that the unit could be supplied complete with Ford's own gearbox, and although this meant that Morgan would have to do away with its remote gearbox mounting, it would be a considerable cost saving compared with the Moss unit used in the Plus 4. The idea also saved production costs because the engine complete with bolted-on gearbox was supplied direct from Ford, and with only a minor alteration, the whole unit dropped neatly into the Plus 4 chassis. However, it did mean that a remote-control gear change had to be designed. This was achieved by extending the normal lever vertically, which in turn was connected to a rod running on a pivot across the scuttle and through the firewall to emerge under the dashboard. The main disadvantage was that the Ford gearbox had only three forward gears. The ratio of the second gear was so low that it sorely restricted acceleration even though there was synchromesh on second and top gears. This arrangement allowed for the use of the umbrella-type handbrake lever that was also mounted under the dashboard. All this meant that the

new model had much more footroom than the Plus 4.

The Morgan company managed to make dramatic savings. In the end, it was able to offer the car at the amazingly low price of £714, compared to £894 for the Plus 4, £939 for a Triumph TR2, or £961 for the MGA.

Introduced at the London Motor Show in October 1955, the 4/4 was listed as a tourer by the factory; its performance was modest by sports car standards—it had less than half the power of the recently fitted TR2 engined Plus 4. There also existed a wide range of moderately priced tuning kits for the 1172 cc Ford Anglia 100E engine for those who wanted more power, while another bonus for the 4/4 buyer was the worldwide availability of Ford service and spare parts.

In September 1957, the company introduced a Competition version of the 4/4. The main mechanical changes were an Aquaplane aluminum alloy cylinder head and inlet manifold, copper and asbestos cylinder head gasket, four-branch exhaust manifold (this raised the compression ratio to 8:1), twin SU carburetors in place of the single Solex carburetor and stronger valve springs. All this increased the power output to 40 bhp at 5100 rpm. There were no body changes made for this model. In all, forty-three Competition models were produced.

Although the 4/4 Series II was only produced as a two-seater, one experimental four-seater was made on chassis number A296. In addition, a drophead coupe was specially built for Miss Skinner, a relative of H.F.S. Morgan, on chassis number A553. This car was finished in yellow and was delivered on February 1, 1960. The Series II model run ended in November 1960.

Prospects

The 4/4 Series II is not particularly sought after by enthusiasts. In comparison with other models, it is rather a pedantic example of the marque. In addition, the gear change and handbrake are more at home in a small family saloon than in a sports car. Those examples fitted with bolt-on tuning accessories and the works' competition model are more desirable, but only by a fraction. Few of the 4/4 Series II model appear on the used car market, and when they do, their prices are not high when compared with other models.

The Standard Special 1267 cc overhead-valve engine was especially designed and produced for Morgan by the Standard Motor Company. A small number were supplied before the war, but it was to power all postwar production 4/4s until the introduction of the Vanguard-engined Plus 4 in 1951. *Morgan Motor Company*

The Competition version of the 4/4 Series II introduced in September 1957, was fitted with an Aquaplane aluminum alloy cylinder head and intake manifold.

This drophead coupe version of the 4/4 Series II was made especially for a relative of H.F.S. Morgan, Miss Skinner. Originally finished in yellow, its chassis number was A553 and engine number Ford 100E B427103C. It is now in the United States and has been slightly modified. The original registration number was 380 AAB.

4/4 Series II	
Engine	Ford 100E
Type	Four cylinders inline
Bore and stroke	63.5 mm x 92.5 mm
Displacement	1172 cc
Valve	Side
Brake horsepower	36 at 4400 rpm
Chassis	Z section steel pressings, underslung, with inverted U section cross-members
Clutch	Borg & Beck single dry plate
Gearbox	Ford three-speed
Final drive	Open Hardy Spicer propeller shaft to Salisbury hypoid-bevel axle unit
Front suspension	Independent with sliding pillars, coil springs with Armstrong telescopic shock absorbers
Rear suspension	Live axle with semi-elliptic springs, and Armstrong piston-type shock absorbers
Brakes	Girling, 9 in. diameter drums, hydraulic, two leading shoes at front, 1¾ in. wide shoes
Wheels	Pressed disc-type with hubcaps, four-stud fitting
Tires	5x16 in., 18 psi front and rear
Dimensions	Wheelbase 96 in., length 144 in., width 56 in., height 50 in., track 47 in.
Weight	Dry 1,568 lb. with 5 gal fuel

When the Morgan factory decided to adopt the Ford 100E Anglia engine for the Series II, it turned out to be a far shrewder move than Morgan had thought. Not only had Morgan adopted a readily available mass-produced unit, but as it turned out, Morgan would benefit from Ford's own intensive and expensive engine development in the future (as Morgan still is). The first development was Ford's introduction of a completely new 105E overhead-valve engine and four-speed gearbox. Although this engine was introduced in a new Anglia in October 1959, Morgan had to negotiate the supply of the new engine. Therefore a year passed before the factory could install the new engine into a new 4/4, the Series III, available in October 1960.

Although only 997 cc displacement, this lightweight, 212 lb. engine had enormous competition potential in the one-liter class, especially as it was linked to Ford's first four-speed gearbox, which had synchromesh on the top three gears. Again, the combined unit dropped neatly into the Morgan chassis, with only a cross-member requiring relocating. The remote gear change remained the same as that used on the Series II.

The 4/4 Series III model is sometimes referred to as the fiftieth anniversary model

The prototype of the 4/4 Series III marked the substitution of the new 997 cc overhead-valve engine fitted to the Ford Anglia for the old 1172 cc Ford side-valve engine. The new series was also fitted with the four-speed, instead of the previous three-speed, gearbox.

because its production coincided with this milestone in the company's history. However, there was no such official designation.

The factory made few external changes, but identification points were different rear lights and the removal of the fasteners for the sidescreens to the outside of the doors. Production continued through November 1961.

Prospects

Although a distinct improvement on the basic Series II, the Series III was also rather pedantic. Once again, it is not sought after in today's used car market, in spite of its comparative rarity value especially in the United Kingdom.

4/4 Series III	
Engine	Ford 105E
Type	Four cylinders inline
Bore and stroke	88.86 mm x 48.41 mm
Displacement	997 cc
Valve	Overhead
Brake horsepower	39 at 5000 rpm
Chassis	Z section steel pressings, underslung, with inverted U section cross-members
Clutch	Single dry plate
Gearbox	Ford four-speed
Final drive	Open Hardy Spicer propeller shaft to Salisbury hypoid-bevel axle unit
Front suspension	Independent with sliding pillars, coil springs with Armstrong telescopic shock absorbers
Rear suspension	Live axle with semi-elliptic springs, and Armstrong piston-type shock absorbers
Brakes	Girling, 9 in. diameter drums, hydraulic, disc front brakes optional extra
Wheels	Pressed disc-type with hubcaps, four-stud fitting
Tires	5.20x15 in.
Dimensions	Wheelbase 96 in., length 144 in., width 56 in., height 50 in., track 47 in.
Weight	Dry 1,568 lb. with 5 gal fuel

4/4 Series IV October 1961- March 1963	

Production of the 4/4 Series III did not last long because production depended entirely on the availability of the Ford 105E engine. In May 1961, Ford upgraded the engine to 1340 cc displacement for use in their new Classic 315 saloon. It was made available to Morgan by October the same year, and the Series IV was born.

The new engine, designated by Ford as the 109E, developed almost forty percent more power than the previous one. This led to several modifications that Morgan needed. More power meant greater performance and the need for greater stopping ability; therefore the eleven-inch disc brakes used on the Plus 4 were adopted as standard. In standard form, the Series IV's improvement in performance over the Series III was substantial; the 0–60 mph time was reduced from 26 to 16.5 seconds, while the top speed went up from 80 mph to 92 mph.

Although the gearbox was essentially the same as for the Series III, it had been altered by Ford to a column change on the Classic 315. Morgan adapted the operating mechanism back, so that its same basic system of operation, the remote gearbox, could still be used.

The model was only produced for eighteen months; its demise in March 1963 was determined once again by the lack of available engines. Ford, by this time, had uprated the engine, making it necessary for Morgan to produce yet another new model.

Prospects

In spite of the retained remote gearbox, the 4/4 Series IV model is far more desirable than the earlier models. Its performance, both in acceleration and top speed, is far more in keeping with everyone's concept of a sports car. In my opinion, it is a collectible model and one that by comparison with other models is still quite cheap—my tip for a good investment.

4/4 Series IV	
Engine	Ford 109E
Type	Four cylinders inline
Bore and stroke	80.96 mm x 65.07 mm
Displacement	1340 cc
Valve	Overhead
Brake horsepower	62 at 5000 rpm
Chassis	Z section steel pressings, under-slung, with inverted U section cross-members
Clutch	Borg & Beck single dry plate
Gearbox	Ford four-speed
Final drive	Open Hardy Spicer propeller shaft to Salisbury hypoid-bevel axle unit
Front suspension	Independent with sliding pillars; coil springs with Armstrong telescopic shock absorbers
Rear suspension	Live axle with semi-elliptic springs, and Armstrong piston-type shock absorbers
Brakes	Girling, 9 in. diameter rear drums, hydraulic, 11 in. disc front brakes
Wheels	Pressed disc-type with hubcaps, four-stud fitting
Tires	5.60x15 in.
Dimensions	Wheelbase 96 in., length 144 in., width 56 in., height 50 in., track 47 in.
Weight	Dry 1,456 lb.

This 1967 4/4 Series IV chassis number B690, was found under a pile of rubble in a contractor's yard in Nigeria in 1974. It has had two owners since and has been restored to fully working condition. In 1977, the President of the Nigeria Motor Sports Club bought the car and still owns it.

4/4 Series V February 1963- March 1968 Competition	★★★ ★★★★

In 1963, once again Ford's upgrading of its engine resulted in a new Morgan model. However, this time the change was to prove to be so successful that the production of the Series V was to last for just over five years, from February 1963 to March 1968. Ford's new engine, designated as the 116E, was developed to power its Cortina saloon and also to make the Classic 315 and the Capri coupe more flexible at the top end of performance. Morgan welcomed the change; it gave the company the shot in the arm that it so badly needed at that time. The new

engine enabled Morgan to offer to the public a sports car that even in standard form could outpace its main rivals: Austin-Healey Sprites, MG Midgets and Triumph Spitfires.

While developing the engine, Ford had also improved its gearbox. The new unit was now fitted with synchromesh on all four gears. This meant that it was slightly larger than the previous unit, but it presented no real problems for fitting it into the Morgan chassis.

Within a few months of the start of production, Morgan offered for an extra £133 a Competition version of the Series V. This was fitted with the Ford Cortina GT engine, which was basically the same as the normal 116E engine, but with a twin-choke Weber carburetor, high-compression cylinder head and a high-lift camshaft. All this increased the power from 65 bhp to 83.5 bhp, with an

SMALL CAR **BIG** performance

95-100 m.p.h. from the FORD 1498 c.c. unit, developing 83.5 B.H.P. at 5,200 r.p.m. Overall weight of car 13¼ cwt. Learn more about this remarkable sports car in the free literature we will gladly send you.

Price £775 inc. P.T.
Wire wheels £39.5.5. extra

Morgan

The Morgan 4/4 Series V COMPETITION MODEL

MORGAN MOTOR CO. LTD., MALVERN LINK, WORCESTERSHIRE.
London: Basil Roy Ltd., 161 Gt. Portland Street, W.1.

Powered by the Ford 116E 1498 cc engine, the 4/4 Series V was in production for just over five years. It was also produced as a Competition model. The price in 1964 was £775 including tax, and wire wheels were £39 extra.

acceleration time from 0–60 mph in 11.9 seconds and a top speed of 95 mph. Towards the end of its production, the Competition model was fitted with an uprated gearbox developed for the Ford Lotus Cortina.

Prospects

The 4/4 Series V is another model that I consider to be a good investment for the future, especially the Competition models. The Series V achieves excellent performance figures when compared with other sports cars of its era and can even give a fair account of itself against much younger cars.

The power unit of the Series V Competition model, complete with twin Weber carburetors. *John H. Sheally II*

4/4 Series V				
Engine	Ford 116E	**Front suspension**	Independent with sliding pillars, coil springs with Armstrong telescopic shock absorbers
Type	Four cylinders inline		
Bore and stroke	80.97 mm x 72.74 mm	**Rear suspension**	Live axle with semi-elliptic springs, and Armstrong piston-type shock absorbers
Displacement	1498 cc		
Valve	Overhead		
Brake horsepower	65 at 4800 rpm, GT engine 83.5 at 5200 rpm	**Brakes**	Girling, 9 in. diameter rear drums, hydraulic, 11 in. disc front brakes
Chassis	Z section steel pressings, underslung, with inverted U section cross-members	**Wheels**	Spoked
		Tires	5.20x15 in. or 155x15 in.
Clutch	Single dry plate	**Dimensions**	Wheelbase 96 in., length 144 in., width 56 in., track 47 in. front, 49 in. rear
Gearbox	Ford four-speed		
Final drive	Open Hardy Spicer propeller shaft to Salisbury hypoid-bevel axle unit	**Weight**	Dry 1,848 lb.

4/4 Ford 1600	
February 1968–	
May 1971	★★★
4/4 Ford GT 1600	
February 1968–	
March 1982	★★★★

In August 1966, Ford introduced the Mark II version of the Cortina, which besides having restyled bodywork was fitted with yet another version of the Kent engine. The displacement was now 1599 cc, and the engine was fitted with a different breathing layout. Now the carburetor and intake manifold were mounted on the left-hand side of the engine (if viewed from the front), whereas previously they had been mounted on top of the exhaust manifold on the right-hand side. The exhaust manifold remained on the right-hand side, and the gases were transferred across the top of the cylinder head, so earning the title of crossflow engine. By February 1968, the engine was available to Morgan and the new 4/4 was introduced. The same gearbox as used on the Series V Competition model still fitted the new engine, so again Morgan had to make few alterations to the chassis to accommodate it.

At the same time, Ford made available a GT version of the engine to Morgan. Designated as 2737E by Ford, it basically had the same modification as did the Series V Competition engine, but with a lightened flywheel and a plastic cooling fan, which helped to further reduce weight. The power difference between the two engines was quite astonishing: 95.5 bhp at 5500 rpm as opposed to 74 bhp at 4750 rpm. With all this extra power available, the Morgan company was able once again to offer a four-seater version in the range. The first produced was chassis number B1732 in September 1968. At an added cost of only £80 including tax, the GT cars created a demand that far exceeded that of the standard version. The ratio was al-

The 4/4 Ford 1600 was in production for just over 13 years. This four-seater had all the weather equipment erected. *Peter Askew*

most four to one. By May 1971, the demand for the GT version was so great that the company phased out the basic engine. From chassis number B2381 (May 1971), all cars produced were fitted with the uprated Ford 2265E, and all engine numbers were prefixed with the letter A. The 2265E engine was the result of Ford's replacement of the 2737E engine with a single overhead camshaft engine for their Series 3 Cortina GT.

In 1970, new exhaust emission control laws in the United States effectively ended Morgan's main export market, the market that had saved the company in the fifties and sixties. Undaunted, Morgan carried out modifications so that its exhaust emission met the requirements of European governments, in particular West Germany. So well was this market developed that by the mid-seventies it became the company's major export market.

Early in 1980, West Germany announced that from April 1982 even stricter exhaust emission regulations would be implemented. This coincided with the fact that Ford had recently developed a completely new engine and transmission, transverse mounted for front-wheel drive. Ford assured Morgan that it was going to continue production of the Kent engine for a considerable time. However, the implications were only too obvious, and with typical shrewdness, Peter Morgan reluctantly decided to end production of the 4/4 Ford 1600. The end of production coincided with the introduction of the new West German regulations in 1982.

Prospects

Examples of the 4/4 Ford 1600 Series, particularly the GT version, retain their value well. The four-seater is ideal for the family man who wants to continue sports car motoring after the children come along. But the 4/4 1600 is not a model which in my opinion will increase in value for many years, although it is a good car to drive and one for which spare parts are easily obtainable. Of course, only early models were imported in the United States, due to the change in exhaust emission regulations.

4/4 Ford 1600	
Engine	Ford 2737E
Type	Four cylinders inline
Bore and stroke	81.00 mm x 77.7 mm
Displacement	1597 cc
Valve	Overhead
Brake horsepower	70 at 4750 rpm
Chassis	Z section steel pressings, underslung cross-members
Clutch	Ford 7½ in. diaphragm-spring clutch
Gearbox	Ford four-speed
Final drive	Open Hardy Spicer propeller shaft to Salisbury hypoid-bevel axle unit
Front suspension	Independent with sliding pillars, coil springs with Armstrong telescopic shock absorbers
Rear suspension	Live axle with semi-elliptic springs, and Armstrong lever-arm shock absorbers
Brakes	Girling, 9 in. diameter rear drums, hydraulic, 11 in. disc front brakes
Wheels	Pressed steel or spoked
Tires	5.60x15 in. on 4J rims or 4½J (spoked) rims
Dimensions	Wheelbase 96 in., length 144 in., width 56 in., track 48 in. front, 48 in. rear
Weight	Dry 1,848 lb. two-seater

4/4 1600 Competition

Specifications are basically the same as for the standard model, but equipped with the Ford 2737GT engine, Weber carburetor and power output of 95.5 bhp at 5500 rpm

---

4/4 Ford GT 1600

From May 1971, chassis number B2381, the Ford 2737GT engine was adopted as standard, all engine numbers for this engine prefixed by letter A. In July 1975, chassis number B3540, a slightly modified version of the same engine was used, but no worthwhile changes can be listed

4/4 Fiat 1600 November 1981– November 1985	★★★
4/4 Ford 1600 CVH March 1982 to date	★★★

After twenty-five years of a continuous supply of Ford engines, Morgan again entered the marketplace to find an engine suitable to power its 4/4 range. Extensive research led Morgan to the Fiat twin-cam engine of 1585 cc, coupled with Fiat's own five-speed gearbox. This engine was well tried and proven, having been in use in various forms since 1966 when it powered the Fiat 124 Sport. After experimenting with one of these engines, the Morgan company decided to go ahead and make an initial purchase.

No sooner had the company committed itself to the Fiat engine, than the Ford CRX engine unexpectedly became available to Morgan. It so happened that at that time a senior Ford executive had a 4/4 on order, and with the announcement of the new engine 4/4, he realized that he would have to accept it with a Fiat engine. He immediately set to work with Morgan to design a method whereby the new four-cylinder CVH (compound valve-angle hemispherical chamber) transverse engine could be adapted for use in the conventional in-line installation.

Not too much work was necessary to effect the change or to fit the engine into the Morgan chassis. The sump was exchanged for the more tapered Cortina equivalent. This coupled with a Capri bellhousing and a Morgan-designed flywheel meant that it could be combined with the Cortina four-speed gearbox. The Cortina gearbox was changed the following year for the newly developed Ford five-speed gearbox designed for the Ford Sierra and Capri models. The

The external appearance of the 4/4 Fiat 1600 and the Ford CVH 1600 were the same. Morgan used this photograph to advertise both models. *Morgan Motor Company*

bulkhead had to be reshaped and new engine mountings designed. Finally, a slightly larger radiator was fitted to improve the cooling. The whole unit worked exceptionally well, and so it was decided to produce the 4/4 with the option of a Fiat or Ford engine, especially as both were powerful enough for the four-seater version.

The side-by-side production of the two variants of the same model was not a particularly satisfactory situation for the efficient working of the factory. This coupled with experiments that were being carried out at that time led Morgan to make a momentous decision. The Fiat-engined 4/4 would be discontinued at the end of the current stock, and a new version of the ever-popular Plus 4 with the Fiat engine would be introduced after a fifteen-year absence.

Soon after production started, the company that supplied Morgan with the steering box gave notice that it had decided that the limited production to meet Morgan's requirements was no longer financially viable and it was going to stop production. Morgan quickly designed and started to produce its own rack-and-pinion steering box. The system was a considerable improvement, but expensive, adding almost £250 to the cost of the car. However, before long a French company named Gemmer started production of a recirculating-ball-type steering box, which proved suitable for installation in the 4/4, at little extra cost to the basic price of the car. The two systems were offered by the factory as options when the car was ordered.

Prospects

The Fiat twin-cam engine cars, produced from November 1981 to November 1985, have great potential for tuning for competition work, but few as yet have appeared in competition. It is a model that could, in the future, become sought after purely for its rarity. However, I feel that it would have to be a long-term investment before any advantage could be gained by selling it.

The 4/4 Ford 1600 CVH powered model retains its value well, and unless it is a particularly poor example, few owners lose much money when they come to sell it. It offers good sports car motoring at compara-

The Fiat 1600 twin-cam engine fitted snugly into the Morgan engine compartment.

The completed rolling chassis of both the Ford CRX-engined 4/4 and the Rover-engined Plus 8s awaited transfer to the bodyshop for the next stage in their construction. No automated production line here, they were physically maneuvered into place by specially employed porters who pushed them around the different workshops by hand. *John H. Sheally II*

tively economical prices. Although not particularly a car to buy for investment purposes, it is a car to own for everyday use.

Production, which started March 1982, continues to date.

4/4 Fiat 1600	
Engine	Fiat T/C 1600
Type	Four cylinders inline
Bore and stroke	84.00 mm x 71.50 mm
Displacement	1584 cc
Valve	Twin overhead camshafts
Brake horsepower	98 at 6000 rpm
Gearbox	Fiat five-speed
Chassis	Z section steel pressings, five boxed or tubular cross-members
Final drive	Open Hardy Spicer propeller shaft to Salisbury hypoid-bevel axle unit
Front suspension	Independent with sliding pillars, coil springs with double acting telescopic shock absorbers
Rear suspension	Live axle with semi-elliptic springs, and Armstrong hydraulic dampers
Brakes	Girling hydraulic dual brake system on four wheels, 9 x 1.75 in. rear drums, hydraulic, 11 in. disc front brakes
Wheels	Pressed steel or spoked
Tires	Radial 175x15 in. or 195/60VR15
Dimensions	Wheelbase 96 in., length 144 in., width 56 in., track 47 in. front, 49 in. rear (increased to length 153 in., width 57 in., track 48 in. front)
Weight	Two-seater 1,624 lb., four-seater 1,680 lb.

4/4 Ford 1600 CVH	
Engine	Ford 1600 CVH
Type	Four cylinders inline
Bore and stroke	79.96 mm x 79.52 mm
Displacement	1597 cc
Valve	Single central overhead cam hydraulic tappets
Brake horsepower	96 at 6000 rpm
Gearbox	Ford four-speed. Changed after a year to Ford five-speed
(Other specifications identical to Fiat 1600 engined 4/4)	

4/4 US Spec	
Engine	1599 cc
Number of cylinders	4
Bore and stroke	81 mm x 77.62 mm
Type of fuel	Propane/butane
Octane	105 plus
Carburetion	Impco 125
Intake manifold	British Ford
Compression ratio	9.0:1
Power	84 DIN SAE at 5500 rpm
Fuel tank capacity	15 gal
Touring range	325-400 miles
Weight (wet)	1,800 lb.
Wheels	Wires or disc

Having been bodied, the cars were wheeled to the paint shop to be finished in the customer's choice of color. Painting was carried out "wing off."

The heart of the present-day 4/4s neatly stacked after arrival from Ford. This illustrates why Morgan engine numbers are not fitted in number sequence.

Chapter 3

Morgan Plus 4

The introduction of the Morgan Plus 4 at the Earls Court Motor Show in October 1950 was to be the start of an era, unprecedented in Morgan history. It was this model that, in all its various forms, changed the face of Morgan and reasserted the marque's authority in motor sport worldwide, even against major manufacturers.

The new model came about as a direct decision made by the chief executive of the Standard Motor Company, Sir John Black (knighted in 1944 for his war work) to adopt a one-engine policy for his passenger-car range. The engine in question, a four-cylinder overhead-valve unit of 2088 cc, was the final specification chosen for the new Standard Vanguard, but its adoption for an enlarged version of the 4/4 range did not come about until other possible sources of engine supply had been examined.

```
Plus 4 flat-radiator
  Feb. 1951-June 1954
Drophead coupe
  four-seater          ★★★★★
Drophead coupe
  two-seater           ★★★★
All others             ★★★
```

Although the engine proposed by Black seemed an apparent logical progression from the specially designed Standard engine used in the 4-4, H.F.S. Morgan was not immediately convinced. Originally, an engine of around 1750 cc had been envisaged for the Vanguard, and when H.F.S. heard of the increase in displacement he sent Peter Morgan out shopping for a possible alternative of not more than 1.75 liter capacity. Only when it was confirmed that no suitable engine of this size was available was the decision made to use the Vanguard engine. The hesitancy on the part of H.F.S. did not construe criticism of the Standard engine. He was concerned lest the government re-impose the prewar system of car taxation, relating the license fee to the number and bore of the cylinders, and the effect this might have on the sales of an over-two-liter Morgan. However, the government adopted a flat-rate taxation, and the Plus 4 was assured of a great reception in the marketplace.

The new car, which was a replacement for rather than a supplement to the 4-4, was offered as a two-seater, four-seater and drophead coupe. In addition, an experimental two-plus-two drophead coupe was built for H.F.S. quite early in the Plus 4's production life (chassis number 2227, engine number V122ME, registration number KNP 152), but such a design was not put into production during the flat-radiator period of the Plus 4.

Although it retained the same basic shape as the 4-4, the Plus 4 body was two inches wider across the cockpit and six inches wider across the pedal boards and gave two inches more legroom. There were also some important changes to the technical specifications

The Vanguard-engined Plus 4 was a logical progression from the 4/4 when the Standard Motor company ceased production of the Special engine. There were few external differences between the two car models, except for the width. The Plus 4 was offered with all three alternative body styles.

to augment the new engine, notably a softer front suspension, made possible by inclining the swivels slightly inward at the top, thereby enabling the vertical length of the pins to be increased, and longer and softer springs to be fitted. Another innovation was the semi-automatic lubrication of the sliding sleeves of the swivels, this being achieved by the driver depressing by foot a valve in the cockpit, which allowed engine oil to be fed under pressure to the bearing surfaces.

The Newton shock absorbers used on the front of the early 4-4s were replaced by Girling double-acting telescopic hydraulic dampers, while Andre frictional shock absorbers previously used at the back had given way to Girling piston-type dampers. The Girling cable brakes had been discarded in favor of a full hydraulic system incorporating nine-inch diameter drums with two leading shoes and with the brake pedal acting directly on the master cylinder.

On its introduction, the two-seater was listed at £510 plus £142.42 purchase tax, while the top-of-the-range drophead coupe was priced at £565 plus £157.69 purchase tax. The Morgans were still competitively placed in the sports car market, despite their considerable increase in power and performance.

Prospects

The Plus 4 flat-radiator model is sought after; prices can only rise as the years progress. With the larger engine and obviously more power, the model is popular, especially as it retains the true prewar sports car image of exposed free-standing radiator and large separate headlamps. Once again, the most popular example is the drophead coupe.

Motoring journalist Peter Garnier of *Autocar* and fellow journalist Charles Heywood compete in Peter Morgan's personal Plus 4 drophead coupe. They gained a silver award in the event.

94

Plus 4 flat-radiator	
Engine	Standard Vanguard
Type	Four cylinders inline
Bore and stroke	85 mm x 92 mm
Displacement	2088 cc
Valve	Overhead
Brake horsepower	68 at 4300 rpm
Chassis	Z section steel pressings, under-slung, with inverted U section cross-members
Clutch	Borg & Beck single dry plate, connected to gearbox by short shaft enclosed in tube
Gearbox	Moss four-speed
Final drive	By open Hardy Spicer 1300 series propeller shaft with needle-bearing universals to hypoid-bevel axle unit Salisbury 3HA23
Front suspension	Independent with sliding stub axle assemblies on near vertical pillars, coil springs with Girling hydraulic telescopic shock absorbers
Rear suspension	Half-elliptic laminated springs, Girling piston-type shock absorbers
Brakes	Girling, hydraulic 9 in. diameter drum, and two leading shoes
Wheels	Pressed disc type with hubcaps, four-stud fitting
Tires	5.25x16 in.
Dimensions	Wheelbase 96 in., length 140 in., (four-seater and coupe 142 in.), width 52 in., (four-seater 54½ in., coupe 50 in.), height to top of screen 46½ in., track 47 in.
Weight	Dry from 1,764 lb.

Morgan introduced the new Plus 4 flat-radiator model with what was then a blaze of publicity. To help in this, the works produced the gleaming show chassis for the car's debut at the Earls Court Motor Show in October 1950. These series of photographs show the remote gearbox, Vanguard engine and Salisbury rear axle. *Morgan Motor Company*

Plus 4 interim and cowled-radiator
    models
    December 1953-May 1958
Drophead coupe
    four-seater   ★★★★★
Drophead coupe interim
    radiator   ★★★★
All others   ★★★

The transformation from the Plus 4 with the upright radiator and separate free-mounted headlamps to the Plus 4 with the cowled radiator (as we know it today) did not happen overnight. It came about through three distinct stages, due to a combination of events. By 1953, motor vehicle designs were beginning to change, with more and more emphasis placed on streamlining and on simplicity of construction. The days of the chromium-plated header tanks and sides of integral radiators and of large free-mounted headlamps were numbered, as more manufacturers "modernized" their designs and manufacturing processes. Although component manufacturers would be willing to supply Morgans, the question was, For how long and at what price? H.F.S. Morgan was only too aware of the fact that before many years the cost of specially made component parts would become prohibitive and that it was therefore only good business practice to adapt his cars' design to accommodate the new mass-produced components.

The first change introduced was to use a small pressurized radiator mounted beneath a curved cowling, with a flat grille and stoneguard set at an angle into it. Pre-focus headlamp units were fitted into semi-recessed nacelles on an inner valance between the cowl and the more generously proportioned fenders. Initially, these headlamps were set quite low. But new lighting regulations effective January 1, 1954, which re-

The introduction of the interim radiator Plus 4 was forced upon the company due to the diminishing availability of the integral radiator and free-standing headlamps. Few of this model were produced. *Morgan Motor Company*

quired a new minimum height above ground to the center of the lamp, necessitated a second change, and so a high lamp version of what is now known as the Plus 4 interim model was created. The production figures of either the low lamp or the high lamp version of this model are unknown; the total number of interim cars produced is also unknown. Another author suggested that the number was only nineteen, and there is no reason to doubt this figure. There is also no reason to believe that there was any change in the works' practice of overlapping design or engine changes.

It is a fact that chassis 3128 is a high lamp version of the interim (the initial change started from chassis number 3000), and according to Derek Day of the factory, the last car produced of this design was chassis 3135. Assuming that this number is correct, then from the works' records we learn that four of this model were fitted with Triumph TR2 engines and the remainder with Standard Vanguard engines.

The interim model was not the happiest of designs. Before long, the third and final stage of change took place, when the curved grille and stoneguard was fitted, which with only minor changes has remained the hallmark of most Morgan models as we know them today.

Initially, the headlamps were quite low, but due to the changes in the lighting regulations in January 1954 the design had to be altered to meet the minimum height requirements. Comparison between this and the previous photograph, illustrates the difference between the high-lamp and low-lamp versions of the Plus 4.

The next change in body style was the fitting of a curved grille and stoneguard, but the Plus 4 model still retained its twin upright spare wheels. *Morgan Motor Company*

The twin upright spares were mounted in the reverse curvature tail end, immediately behind the fuel tank. The outline of the tank was no longer visible. The white-faced instruments on the dash were standard on the early Plus 4s, but changed later in the production run. *Morgan Motor Company*

This Vanguard-engined two-seater was originally built as a flat-radiator model and left the works in August 1954, the next-to-last flat-radiator made. When it was not sold by the main agent within the year, the car was returned to the works in August 1955. Morgan rebodied it as a cowled-radiator model and resold it to another agent in October 1955. This happened to quite a few of the last flat-radiator Plus 4s, as the public preferred the new shape.

The Plus 4 was produced in many variants over the years and was to undergo many changes within each example. The change to the cowled radiator was a major one; the other major body style change was the eventual doing away with the twin upright spare wheels (except for on the drophead coupe which had one), which had been a feature of the Morgan since 1936. They were replaced with a single spare wheel mounted partially in and at the same angle as the sloping rear panel.

Prospects

In spite of their rarity, the few Plus 4 interim and cowled-radiator models that survive do not fetch as high prices as might be expected. After the transition, the first cowled-radiator models retained the twin upright spare wheels, and these cars are popular in today's market. Rarely found on the open market, they are usually sold between enthusiasts. All examples of the Plus 4 interim and cowled-radiator models can only increase in price.

The same cowled-radiator Plus 4 with the hood erected. The overall lines of this model, to me, represent the ideal compromise between old and new body styles. *Morgan Motor Company*

Due to the limited number of Plus 4 four-seater drophead coupes made, they have become a collector item. Externally, the differences between this model and the two-seater were apparent in the hood. The four-seater had a squarer look, to give headroom for the rear seat passengers. Another difference was the distance from the rear of the door to the start of the hood bottom trim. Also, there was a small protruding trunk on the four-seater. *John H. Sheally II*

In the heyday of the Morgan three-wheelers, the Family model proved deservedly popular, and perhaps the closest we have seen to a family four-wheeled Morgan is the variant of the Plus 4 that was announced in 1954. At £879, the four-seater drophead coupe was the most expensive car in Morgan's range. Weighing eighty-four pounds more than the Plus 4 four-seater tourer, the new Plus 4's performance was restricted by comparison. Even so, this did not prevent examples being used in competition; one owned by T. Dixon-Smith was sufficiently impressive to be described in the motoring press as "being indecently quick."

Two prototype cars were produced in 1951 and 1953, with the then current flat radiator, although subsequently both cars were rebodied with cowled radiators. The 1953 car became the personal property of H.F.S. Morgan, who used it until his death in 1959; it was then eventually sold to a buyer in the United States.

The bodywork of the four-seater differed from that of the two-seater drophead coupe mainly at the rear, with a single spare wheel being hidden in a small luggage compartment. Other differences were in the size of the door windows, which were larger, and in the hood and hood frame. In addition, there was an option of either a 4:1 or 3.73:1 ratio rear axle.

All cars sold in the United Kingdom were fitted with the Vanguard engine, while export cars were fitted with the twin-carburetor Triumph TR2 engine. All cars were fitted with Moss gearboxes.

Only fifty-one cars were produced with this bodywork, including the two prototypes. Twenty-nine were destined for the UK market, eighteen for the United States, two for Spain, and one each for Belgium and Australia.

Prospects

This rare model is most sought after among enthusiasts, who have invented the name Snobmog for all variations of this model. The Plus 4 four-seater drophead coupe commands high prices, if and when one comes on to the market. However, do not completely despair, because the current whereabouts of fifteen of these cars is unknown. There is still an outside chance of finding one that is being used as a chicken coop or the like, if you are lucky. The Plus 4 four-seater drophead coupe can only increase in value.

The four-seater drophead coupe had a small luggage compartment and a large hood and hood frame. This car was originally exported to the United States, but is now owned by Fred Myer, president of the Austrian Morgan Club. *Roger Moran*

101

The first car fitted with the Triumph TR2 engine was a flat-radiator model of the Plus 4, but this car was eventually rebodied as a cowled-radiator model by the works. The Triumph TR2 engine was first offered as an option to the public in October 1953, but it was not until April 1954 that it became standard. Production of the Vanguard engine version was phased out as the stock of engines was used up. Initially, the prefix letters P for Vanguard engines and T for TR engines were used with the chassis numbers, but this was dropped after the Vanguard engine ceased to be available.

The introduction of the TR2 engine in September 1954 meant that, at approximately £830, the Plus 4 was the cheapest car available on the British market able to reach the magic 100 mph, although testers found the last two or three miles per hour took a long time to achieve. The TR2 engine was fitted through June 1958.

Prospects

Prices of this Plus 4 Triumph TR2 engined model reflect the rarity of the particular example, with once again the four- or two-seater drophead coupe commanding the highest. Well worth purchasing if one comes on the market, this Plus 4 model can only increase in value. Especially interesting are the rare cars fitted with twin upright spare tires.

Plus 4 Triumph TR2 engined	
Engine	Triumph TR2
Type	Four cylinders inline
Bore and stroke	83 mm x 92 mm
Displacement	1991 cc
Valve	Overhead
Brake horsepower	90 at 4800 rpm
Carburetor	Twin SU
Chassis	Z section steel pressings, under-slung, with inverted U section cross-members
Clutch	Borg & Beck 9 in. single dry plate, connected to gearbox by short shaft enclosed in tube
Gearbox	Moss four-speed
Final drive	Open Hardy Spicer propeller shaft with needle-bearing universals to hypoid-bevel axle unit
Front suspension	Independent with sliding stub axle assemblies on near vertical pillars, coil springs with Girling telescopic shock absorbers
Rear suspension	Semi-elliptic laminated springs, Girling hydraulic shock absorbers, and Silentbloc bushes
Brakes	Girling hydraulic 9 in. drums with two leading shoes front and rear
Wheels	Pressed steel with hubcaps
Tires	5.25x16 in.
Dimensions	Wheelbase 96 in., length 140 in., width 56 in., height 51 in., track 47 in.
Weight	Dry 1,848 lb.

Charlie Curtis, the works' chief tester until he retired in the early 1970s, prepared Peter Morgan's early TR-engined Plus 4 rally car KUY 387 for a rally. The white tape on the fender was an indicator to help in stopping astride lines, which was usual in special tests. *Morgan Motor Company*

The Plus 4 Triumph TR3 engined model was introduced in March 1956 at just under £894 and was outwardly identical to the TR2 engined model that it replaced. However, beneath the bonnet the difference became evident: the TR3 engine was fitted with larger carburetors and a different intake manifold. This powerful engine helped lift the car's top speed to 105 mph and improved the acceleration times, although fuel consumption, which had been a strong point with the TR2 engine, suffered. Morgan fitted the TR3 model through February 1964.

Prospects

The Plus 4 TR3 is yet another model that can only increase in value, but few come on the open market—a good investment.

Plus 4 Triumph TR3 engined	
Engine	Triumph TR3
Type	Four cylinders inline
Bore and stroke	83 mm x 92 mm
Displacement	1991 cc
Valve	Overhead
Brake horsepower	100 at 5000 rpm
Compression ratio	8.5:1
Carburetors	Twin SU H6
(All other specifications as for TR2 engined cars)	

The drophead coupe's hood could open in three positions. This coupe de ville position was popular with owners. *John H. Sheally II*

The TR3 engine, introduced in 1956, had significantly more power than the TR2 engine. The intake and exhaust manifolds were separate castings and were quite independent of one another. The special intake manifold was constructed in two halves joined by a balance pipe. *Morgan Motor Company*

This beautifully restored 1963 Plus 4 belongs to Edgar L. Berre, Jr., of Ohio. Wire wheels were on offer as an optional extra and, to me, improve the overall appearance of the model greatly.

Plus 4 Triumph TR4 and
   TR4A engined models
   other than special
   models
   October 1962-
   January 1969   ★★★★

With the introduction in 1962 of the TR4 engine, the Triumph and Morgan sports cars were moved into the over-two-liter class, but performance was considerably enhanced, especially when the increase in capacity was followed by a further increase in power for the TR4A. This was to be the last of the Morgan Plus 4s for many years. It was a model that enjoyed, and indeed continues to enjoy, a fine competition record. Any variant of this Plus 4 is greatly sought after by enthusiasts, and their prices reflect this.

The TR4 was introduced in October 1962 and the TR4A as an option in 1966, and they were priced from £816. Morgan built them until January 1969.

Prospects

Like the TR3, the Plus 4 TR4 is destined to appreciate.

The TR 4 engine in Berre's Plus 4 retained the SU carburetors, but twin Stromberg's were also an option.

Plus 4 Triumph TR4 and TR4A engined	
Engine	Triumph TR4 or TR4A
Type	Four cylinders inline
Bore and stroke	86 mm x 92 mm both engines
Displacement	2138 cc
Valve	Overhead
Brake horsepower	TR4: 100 at 4600 rpm
	TR4A: 104 at 4700 rpm
Carburetors	Twin Stromberg or SU
Brakes	Girling hydraulic, 11 in. front discs and 9 in. rear drums
Wheels	Spoked
Tires	Dunlop 5.60x15 in. or 165x15 in.
Dimensions	Wheelbase 96 in., length 144 in., width 56 in., track 47 in. front, 49 in. rear
(All other specifications as for TR2 engined cars)	

Carrying luggage in a Morgan was always a
problem no matter which model. The owner of
this Plus 4 has overcome the problem in a novel
manner. *John H. Sheally II*

The designation Super Sports has traditionally been reserved by the Morgan factory to denote a model capable of exceptional competition performance. The adoption of this name for a special version of the Plus 4 model came about purely as a result of the tuning skills and competition successes of one man, Chris Lawrence.

When Lawrence decided in late 1957 to try just one more season in racing, he and his fiancee pooled all their savings to buy a 1956 Morgan Plus 4. For the previous eight years, Lawrence had competed on a shoestring with various makes of cars and in many forms of racing, with only limited success,

but his decision to buy the Plus 4 was to change his life. A competent amateur engine-tuner, he spent many long hours studying and working on the Plus 4 to obtain the maximum power possible from the engine.

In the fifties, the best way for an unknown driver to make his name was in marque racing, now called modsports racing. Marque racing was for certain specified types of car only; these included the AC Ace, Austin-Healey, MGA, Morgan Plus 4 and Triumph TR series. Twenty-two races for these cars were arranged throughout the season for the Freddie Dixon Trophy. The first race of the 1958 series was held at Aintree, and Lawrence found that he had many teething troubles, finishing last. Undeterred, he persevered, and by the end of the season he had broken the lap record for marque racing.

The classic Plus 4 lines! This original 1967 US export model had wire wheels and black-faced dials (which were by then standard on the model). Note the tail and rear indicator lamps; these were to change later, replaced by the stalk fitting used today. *John H. Sheally II*

By 1959, he had learned much, and when he started his first full competition season in the Plus 4 car, he was satisfied with his results. He took part in virtually every marque race, and most of his wins were to be runaways. In all, he had five outright wins, four seconds and one third. The following year was to be a sensational one. At the start of the season, he entered all twenty-two races in the Freddie Dixon Trophy series— and almost unbelievably won twenty-one of them and was placed third in the other, resulting in an unprecedented win of the trophy. Next, he extended his racing onto the major racetracks of Europe.

In 1961, he entered his Plus 4 in the 1,000 km race at Nurburgring; although Lawrence did not finish, he broke the Porsche-held two-liter record. The Germans were so intrigued by this "curious machine which only seemed to spend a quarter of the race on the ground," that they presented Lawrence with a special award. He followed this performance by an excellent second overall in the Grand Prix de Spa in Belgium, and then he went on to Le Mans where he was entered in the twenty-four-hour race. When he presented his car to the French scrutineers, they refused it entry as they were convinced that the Plus 4 was a prewar car that had been fitted with disc brakes. Undaunted, Lawrence went on to Monza to compete in the Coppa International Europa, where he came second overall.

Peter Morgan was not slow to realize that it was not only Lawrence's ability to drive the car well but also his skill in tuning to obtain absolute maximum performance from the engine that made him so successful. So impressed was Peter Morgan that by late 1960 the factory entered into an agreement with Lawrence, whereby he prepared a few engines on a regular basis for the Morgan works for those customers looking for an extra special performance car. Although at that time the cars were not designated as Super Sports, they were later to receive the name (even without the low-line body of later cars).

Working with Chris Lawrence had been a particularly bold step for Peter Morgan to take. It must be remembered that all this happened before the days of the Mini-Cooper and Lotus-Cortina. Nowadays we are used to manufacturers fitting their cars with engines prepared by specialist companies, but in 1960 and 1961, the Morgan Motor Company was the only one.

As a result of obtaining this regular order from the Morgan factory, Lawrence opened up a small workshop at Westerham Motors, Acton, London, and the now famous Lawrencetune company was formed. Here, he race-tuned Triumph TR series engines not only for the Morgan factory and Morgan owners, but also for the occasional Triumph owner.

The refusal to accept the Morgan for the Le Mans twenty-four-hour race upset Peter Morgan. Besides any matter of hurt pride, there was also the effect it would have on sales. Obviously, a success in the race would be a great help to the company's falling sales figures and also would restore the marque's international good name, particularly in France. Morgan therefore decided to give full works' support to Lawrence, including a complete rebodying of the car with a low-line 4/4 body, which it was reasoned would result in a substantial reduction in drag and weight. The lowering was achieved easily because of the reduced height of the engine when fitted with side-mounted Weber carburetors. So was born the first Super Sports, although the actual production model differed in many ways from the specially prepared race car.

In 1962, Lawrence repeated the second overall at Spa, followed by a magnificent class win at Le Mans. Partnered by Richard Shepherd-Baron, Lawrence and the car finished thirteenth overall, among only eighteen finishers, and covered 2,255 miles at an average speed of 93.97 mph. Chris Lawrence and the Morgan Motor Company had been vindicated.

When the Plus 4 Super Sports model was announced late in 1961, it offered arguably the best value in terms of performance available at that time anywhere. With acceleration figures of 0–60 mph in 7.8 seconds and 0–100 mph in 22.8 seconds, it was tailor-made for competition and was to earn count-

Chris Lawrence knew that he must prove himself and his engine tuning by being successful on the racetrack. Here he lapped an MG in the British Automobile Racing Club members' meeting at Goodwood on March 23, 1959. He was first in the marque race in the car that was to win its class at Le Mans in 1962. *Chris Lawrence*

A second Morgan was brought from the works and tuned to Chris Lawrence's specifications. Here the car, XRX 1, competed in the Coppa Inter-Europa at Monza in 1961. The experimental hardtop was in the end manufactured and offered for sale to all Plus 4 Super Sports owners. *Chris Lawrence*

less successes. These figures were comparable to those of the Plus 8 when it was introduced.

Engines for the Super Sports were sent from the factory to Lawrence's workshop, where they received the Lawrencetune treatment. The workshop team completely stripped the engine and sent the clutch, flywheel, connecting rods and crankshaft to Jack Brabham (Motors Ltd.) for balancing. While this was happening, Lawrence's team polished and gas-flowed the cylinder head. The compression ratio was raised to 9:1, and a high-lift camshaft was fitted. At the same time, the engine was given a cast alloy intake manifold, while a pair of either 42 or 45 DCOE Weber carburetors was added. A specially designed four-branch exhaust manifold was also fitted. The engine developed initially 115 bhp at 5500 rpm, but later this was increased to 125 bhp at the same rpm.

The engine was then returned to the factory, where it was fitted to a standard Plus 4 chassis, which in turn was covered with a light alloy low-line 4/4 body and fenders (this style of body was adopted for all Plus 4s as of September 1966). Seventy-two-spoke wide rim wheels were fitted. Many examples were fitted with individual bucket seats in place of the conventional bench-back seats. Finally, an oil cooler was mounted in front of the radiator, but behind the grille. The total weight of the car was 1,736 lb. compared with 1,884 lb. of the normal Plus 4.

Prospects

Of all the Morgan models produced over the years, the Plus 4 Super Sports must be regarded as the most sought after by enthusiasts. Any example, regardless of condition, commands a high price. Obviously the better the condition, the higher the price. The car is everything expected of a classic sports car; it looks the part and can out-perform most of its contemporaries and a large number of modern sports cars.

The Plus 4 Super Sports was produced mainly to order until May 1968, and in all 104 were built, including five four-seaters and four drophead coupes. Several other

Chris Lawrence competed in the Brands Hatch races on May 10, 1959. He was first in the marque race. In that season, he won nine marque races and one handicap race, finished second four times and third once, finishing in every race. He certainly proved himself. *Chris Lawrence*

Plus 4s were fitted with Lawrencetune engines, but the factory does not recognize them as being Super Sports for various reasons.

Plus 4 Competition
October 1965-
April 1967

During the production of the Plus 4 Super Sports, the factory received enquiries as to the possibility of a cheaper version of this competition car being made available to the public. In 1965, the factory responded to the demand by introducing the Plus 4 Competition model. Its price was nearly £100 dearer than for the ordinary two-seater, but considerably cheaper than for the Super Sports priced at £1,150 (by far the most expensive of the range). Priced at £938 including tax, the Competition model was dubbed the poor man's Super Sports.

The low-line body was virtually the same as that of the Super Sports, with only a few minor differences. With the same 2138 cc Triumph TR4 engine as used in the ordinary Plus 4, extra power was obtained by fitting it with the four-branch free-flow exhaust system used on the Super Sports. Wire wheels were standard, but not the special wide rim seventy-two-spoke variety.

Prospects

Morgan announced the Plus 4 Competition model in October 1965 at the Earls Court Motor Show. It made only forty-two of this model; the car was produced only to

The Plus 4 Super Sports can immediately be recognized from the front by the air intake for the Weber carburetors on the right-hand side of the bonnet (as viewed from the driver's seat).
John H. Sheally II

111

The TR4 and TR4A engines used in the Plus 4 Super Sports were sent to Chris Lawrence's to receive the Lawrencetune treatment. Basically, this was stripping down the engine, balancing all internal moving parts, polishing and gas-flowing the cylinder head, and fitting a modified inlet manifold and a pair of Weber carburetors. *John H. Sheally II*

Although the speedometer of this car has been personalized while the instruments were being restored, this is an original dashboard of a Super Sports. *John H. Sheally II*

order and only in two-seater form. The last car left the factory in April 1967. One car was used by the factory; fifteen were sold in the United Kingdom; eleven went to the United States; four to Canada; three to France; two each to Germany and Sweden; and one each to Australia, Belgium, Panama and Switzerland.

Examples of this model rarely come on the market, but when they do they command only slightly less than the Plus 4 Super Sports. A sound investment.

The rear axle compartment of the Super Sports also housed the two six-volt batteries. The handbrake operating rods and compensator have remained basically the same throughout four-wheeler production. *John H. Sheally II*

Front disc brakes and rear drum brakes were standard on all Super Sports. *John H. Sheally II*

The first, and so far the only, fully enclosed Morgan produced at the Malvern factory was the Plus 4 Plus. Possibly the most controversial of all Morgan models, it received a mixed reception when it was introduced at the 1963 Earls Court Motor Show. Some of the motoring press described the closed fiberglass body as having a Jaguar XK150 front and a Lotus Elite rear, while die-hard Morgan purists were almost lost for words—and those words that they did find could never be printed. This was the final blow as far as they were concerned. It had been bad enough when ten years earlier their "true sports car" had been "sissified" because it was fitted with a cowled-radiator grille. But this was beyond belief.

For several years prior to the introduction of this model, Peter Morgan had been considering the possibility of introducing a fiberglass-bodied, fully enclosed Morgan. He had discussed the idea at great length with his father; however H.F.S. had been reluctant to produce such a model, preferring to wait until fiberglass had stood the test of time on other vehicles. One of his main objections was the whippiness of the Morgan chassis; this he reasoned would cause cracking to the body.

In 1962, after making a detailed study of a Debonair S1 Ford special (similar to the one fitted to Roy Clarkson's well tried and successful rally car of the mid-fifties), Peter Morgan contacted the manufacturers E. B. Plastics Ltd. of Tunstall, Stoke-on-Trent. E. B. Plastics was by no means a small back-street company; besides their sports car activities, they also produced cabs for Foden and ERF trucks and Austin-Parkinson electric vehicles, plus varied fiberglass moldings for the motor industry in general.

Peter Morgan asked E. B. Plastics if it could produce a body similar to that of the Debonair for the Morgan Plus 4 chassis, but insisted that some of the Morgan's classic lines be retained. The new body must keep the Morgan front appearance and incorporate a somewhat similar radiator grille. He also insisted that there be no overhang at the front and that no mechanical changes be made to the chassis. So successful was E. B. Plastics in keeping to these specifications that the only chassis change necessary was a pair of sheet steel extensions, which were bolted on each side of the engine and which linked the front suspension mounting to the bulkhead. The result was a much sturdier structure. It was hoped that this would remove the risk of cracking of the body due to chassis flexing.

The founder and managing director of E. B. Plastics, John N. Edwards, designed and produced working drawings of several variations on the Debonair theme. After discussion, Peter Morgan selected one to put into production, but before the final go-ahead was given, a scale model of the proposal was submitted for approval. Coincidentally, a few years ago another model at about one-fifth scale of a fiberglass-bodied Morgan was discovered. It was apparently another inspection piece made by another company who was also contacted to submit designs.

Next, a full-scale pattern was made, using wood formers, and this was paneled in light alloy, on which many hours were spent producing a high-quality cellulose finish. The first mold was made from epoxy resin, and while the body was being prepared, Peter Morgan sent the next laid down Plus 4 chassis from the production line to the Tunstall works. He was determined that the new body be fitted on a standard Plus 4 chassis, without any special alterations other than those stated as necessary. In this way, the new model could be produced without interruption to normal production. The body was mounted, cellulosed, fitted with lights and other necessary equipment, and trimmed. This prototype was fitted with a pair of individual seats with a common bench back, but all subsequent cars of this model were supplied with bucket seats. The prototype was also the only one produced in this way; all other cars were finished, cellulosed and trimmed back at the Morgan factory after the body had been fitted at the Tunstall works.

This is one of the experimental body designs submitted for consideration before the final Plus 4 Plus design was settled on. This design was made by E. B. Plastics Ltd., whose alternative design Peter Morgan finally accepted. The car, found in need of restoration in 1978, is now fully restored and is owned by a West German enthusiast.

When complete, the prototype was registered as 869 KAB and collected from E. B. Plastics by Peter Morgan personally. Then began extensive road testing, including a tour of Spain and France. The tests revealed a problem associated with the stiff front end of the car, which meant that the front suspension was working harder than with the usual flexing chassis, which absorbed some of the shock. In spite of this, the new model still retained the Morgan road-holding capabilities. John Bolster, when he test drove the prototype for *Autosport* in 1963, noted that "in a veritable cloud burst, I drove along Ross Spur in sheets of spray, reaching 105 m.p.h. The famous controlability of the Morgan was fully in evidence, fast curves being taken at speed in complete confidence . . . the car rides better than previous examples of the marque because the ridged chassis ensures that the springs do more work." He was also impressed by its maximum speed of around 110 mph and consumption figures of about 29 mpg.

Like all new Morgans, the Plus 4 Plus was entered in competitions as a way of proving the model. Driven by Peter Morgan, the car performed well in both rallies and trials. These results went a long way in dispelling the main doubts of the cars' critics.

Prospects

In spite of this and the fact that the car had been quite well received by the motoring press, public reaction was less satisfactory, and the model was produced only spasmodically over the next four years. Now twenty-five years later, the Plus 4 Plus fixed head coupe is regarded as a collector piece, and the occasional one that comes on the market commands a price that reflects its rarity and collectibility. In all, only twenty-six and two spare bodies of this model were made, including the prototype, the remains of which are still kept at the factory after an accident.

Plus 4 Plus fixed-head coupe	
Engine	Triumph TR4
Type	Four cylinders inline
Bore and stroke	86 mm x 92 mm
Displacement	2138 cc
Valve	Overhead
Brake horsepower	105 at 4750 rpm
Carburetor	Twin Stromberg CD
Chassis	Z section steel pressings, underslung, with inverted U section cross-members
Clutch	Borg & Beck 9 in. single dry plate, connected to gearbox by short shaft enclosed in tube
Gearbox	Moss four-speed
Final drive	Open Hardy Spicer 1300 series propeller shaft with needle-bearing universals to hypoid-bevel axle unit
Front suspension	Independent with sliding stub axle assemblies on near vertical pillars, coil springs with Armstrong telescopic shock absorbers
Rear suspension	Half-elliptic laminated springs, Armstrong lever-arm shock absorbers
Brakes	Girling, hydraulic 11 in. front discs, and 9 in. rear drums with 1¾ in. wide shoes
Wheels	72 spoked
Tires	5.60x15 in.
Dimensions	Wheelbase 96 in., length 152 in., width 61 in., height 51 in., track 47½ in. front, 49 in. rear
Weight	Dry 1,820 lb.

The wooden former on which the fiberglass bodies of the Plus 4 Plus were constructed at the Tunstall Works of E. B. Plastics. *J. N. Edwards*

Although the design was not well accepted by the motoring public when it was introduced, the Plus 4 Plus is now a collector car and is a most sought after model. This US example was fully restored by John H. Sheally II, the renowned US Morgan enthusiast. The UK car belongs to C. (Sammy) Sampson, who owns two other Morgans including a three-wheeler. *John H. Sheally II*

An accident repair in England of one of the fiberglass Plus 4 Plus bodies resulted in its Swedish owner Ingvar Fredriksson visiting the Morgan factory. He managed to buy one of the spare bodies (none are left now). This was how he transported them back to Sweden.

Ancient and modern. *John H. Sheally II*

SLR Morgan 1963-64	★★★★★

The Sprinzel Lawrence Racing Morgans were designed and developed as a direct result of Chris Lawrence's successes at Le Mans, Spa, Monza and elsewhere in the early sixties. In order to remain competitive in the mid-sixties, he needed a faster car than his basically standard-bodied Morgans, and late in 1963 he was offered a new Porsche 904. He remained loyal to Morgan, however, and so used the TR4 engined Plus 4 as the basis for a new car.

Lawrence had tuned a couple of rally cars for John Sprinzel, which had proved quite successful, and after some discussion the two drivers teamed up to form Sprinzel Lawrencetune Racing. Sprinzel managed to obtain some financial support from British Petroleum, and this, together with money put in by each party, plus definite orders for two cars, provided sufficient finance to begin development.

The regulations governing Group 4 GT racing at that time allowed for body modifications provided that the weight of the original car was not cut by more than fifteen percent. The aerodynamic body of the SLR was designed jointly by Sprinzel and Lawrence, and was made in aluminum by Williams and Pritchard, and attached to the bare chassis with light sub-frames. No drastic chassis modifications were required, but a small amount of strengthening was done to the transverse bulkhead, and sub-frames were provided for mounting the shock absorbers.

Three cars were to be built on Morgan chassis and one on Neil Dangerfield's ex-Sid Hurrell Triumph TR4 (SAH 137), which had run so well at Monza in 1963. One of the Morgans was the works' prototype of the Plus 4 Super Sports (170 GLP); this car was an exact replica of Lawrence's Le Mans car, for which it had acted as back-up.

The modified TR4 engine had a new cross-flow cylinder head with staggered ninety-degree angled valves, a development financed jointly by Lawrencetune and the

Morgan Motor Company, but which was never completed. This cylinder head was reported in the motoring press to be a Blunstien head; this was true but only in a round-about way. Bill Blunstien worked for Lawrencetune and produced the casting drawings but the design was mainly Lawrence's work. Several problems were encountered concerning the lubrication of the rockers, and another irritation was the oiling up of the 10 mm spark plugs, which had a narrow heat band. As Lawrence explained, "If you could get on the front row of the grid and could get away at the start you were alright. Otherwise, the plugs nearly always oiled up." Another complication of this cylinder head on the two-liter engine was that the valves were so large that it was impossible to obtain a compression ratio of 10:1, which it was felt would be ideal. Instead, the compression ratio was a modest 6.8:1, but even so the engine developed more torque than the standard engine.

The cars also had larger stub axles and steel hubs, which had been developed as a result of numerous breakages in the 1961 and 1962 seasons. During this period, the Lawrencetune-prepared race cars developed such a high g factor that the standard hubs could not take the strain, something which the manufacturers were at first reluctant to accept, although in due course they were persuaded to change the material and increase the size. The stronger hubs were fully race-proved and have since been adopted as standard equipment for the Plus 8.

Prospects

The SLR Morgans achieved some notable competition successes, and Chris Lawrence used one to lower the class lap record at Goodwood from one minute forty-two seconds to one minute thirty-nine seconds, then went on to take a brilliant third place overall at Spa, between six Porsche 904s, which could never have been described as road cars.

At least two of the three Morgans and the Triumph still exist and are well documented. From time to time, the cars are still seen in action, giving a good account of themselves, and one wonders how much they might have achieved had not Lawrence suffered a

serious road accident in 1964, which prevented any further development of the SLRs.

Should one of these three cars ever come on to the market, the owner could name the price. A must for the serious investor.

The SLR (Sprinzel Lawrence Racing) was a successful exercise in giving a racing Plus 4 Morgan a more aerodynamic shape. However, when it first appeared in marque races, it created much controversy, from competitors and organizers. This car, in the rain at Silverstone, was at the Bentley Driver's Club meeting in 1976, where it was still competitive on the track. *Charles J. Smith*

Early in 1985, Fiat offered Morgan a two-liter fuel-injected engine. Maurice Owen, Morgan's Research & Development engineer felt that this engine had great potential as a mid-stream alternative between the basic 4/4 and the high-performance Plus 8.

Having acquired one of the engines, Owen found that it fitted into the Morgan chassis with the minimum of alterations. Using the fuel tank that he had developed for use with the Rover Vitesse V-8 engine in the Plus 8, he was able to overcome one of the difficulties. He also found that the wiring harness, which he had also developed to accommodate the complicated electrics in the Vitesse injection system, required only the minimum of modification to be incorporated into the new car. The five-speed gearbox of the Fiat 125 Special completed the power chain.

Developing 122 bhp, the new car was clearly too powerful to still retain the 4/4 designation. The company's board of directors decided to revive one of the most respected designations in Morgan history—the Plus 4.

The extra power also meant that it would be advisable to have more tire area presented to the road surface. The Morgan Plus 4 was therefore fitted with six-inch wire wheels, with Avon tires as standard, making it the only car in the world with low-profile tires fitted to wire wheels. This in turn meant that the fenders had to be slightly widened to accommodate the tires.

The model remained in production until January 1987, when production ended because the supplier converted to transverse engine installation for front-wheel drive. This, in turn, also led to the supplier's changing its gearbox to column change only, which was not convertible for use in the Morgan. Initially, fifteen Plus 4s were made with the twin-cam 2000 cc engine but fitted with a 36/38 DCOE Weber twin-choke carburetor, before Morgan began to make the fuel-injection version.

Prospects

It is hard to predict the possible investment value of the Plus 4 Fiat-engined model. Although the fuel-injected version has the edge on performance, I feel that any of the fifteen cars fitted with carburetors could, after some years, become a collector model—but don't hold your breath.

Plus 4 Fiat-engined	
Engine	Fiat 2000, fuel-injection
Type	Four cylinders inline
Bore and stroke	84 mm x 90 mm
Displacement	1995 cc
Valve	Twin overhead camshafts belt-driven, two valves per cylinder
Brake horsepower	122 at 5300 rpm
Carburetor	Bosch LE Jetronic Injection System with Digiplex Control
Chassis	Z section steel pressings, five boxed or tubular cross-members
Gearbox	Fiat five-speed
Final drive	Open Hardy Spicer propeller shaft to Salisbury hypoid-bevel axle unit
Front suspension	Independent with sliding pillars, coil springs with double acting tubular shock absorbers
Rear suspension	Live axle with semi-elliptic springs, and Armstrong hydraulic-type shock absorbers
Brakes	Girling dual system, 9 in. x 1¾ in. diameter rear drums, 11 in. disc front brakes
Wheels	Center laced 6x15 in. wire
Tires	195/60Rx15 Avon Turbo Speed Radial
Dimensions	Wheelbase 96 in., length 153 in., width 57 in., track 47 in. front, 49 in. rear, height 50 in.
Weight	Dry 1,870 lb.

Morgan Plus 4
2-seater & 4-seater

A famous name returns. Based on the current 4/4 1600 and available as a 2-seater or 4-seater, the Plus 4 is fitted with the Fi[at?] 2-litre petrol injected engine. The car is some 3" wider than the 1600 and has 6" wire wheels fitted as standard.

The Morgan factory has used British engines to power its production models wherever possible. The need to depart from this tradition when Morgan introduced the Fiat-engined 4/4s and the Plus 4s did not feel right to either the company or Morgan enthusiasts, although the cars sold well enough. It must therefore have been quite a relief to the Morgan company when the Austin/Rover Group introduced their award-winning M16 Lean-burn sixteen-valve fuel-injected two-liter engine—especially when Morgan was to negotiate a supply of these engines converted for in-line running. The conversion produced one major problem, and this was the marriage of the engine to the Rover 75 mm five-speed gearbox, as fitted to the Plus 8. It was necessary to make modifications to the bellhousing, scuttle and chassis cross-members to accommodate it. This problem was overcome, and the new model became a practical venture.

The new model was to be in addition to the range, rather than a replacement. And rather than create a new model designation, Morgan decided to use the world-famous Plus 4. As the Morgan company said in its press release on the model, "The Morgan Plus 4 is re-born with a British 16 valve, 2 litre engine."

Until the introduction of this new model at Brands Hatch racetrack on May 3, 1988, no new Morgan model, as far as I have been able to ascertain, had ever had an official press launch. When questioned about this at the launch, Peter Morgan's son and heir apparent to the dynasty, Charles Morgan said, "Well, there have been so many rumours and stories about the new car that we thought we would use the occasion to announce that production has now started."

The first prototype was produced on chassis number 7,300, registration number D 955 AWP. This was a specially constructed four-seater. Aluminum bodied, the car was basically a marriage between a two- and a four-seater 4/4 body. The front of the car, up to and including the modified scuttle and windscreen, was a two-seater with a Plus 8 cowl. The rear was the modified four-seater body. The resulting body was an acceptable combination of the two, and it was doubtful if the union would be noticed by more than a handful of Morgan enthusiasts. The car was finished in opalescent white, with pale blue interior, dark blue tonneau cover and a burr wood dashboard. The second prototype was built on chassis number 7,400, registration number E 766 FUY. This was bodied as a two-seater, similar to the 4/4 body, with only slight modifications. It was steel bodied and finished in dark metallic blue, with a red interior and tonneau cover, and red wire wheels.

The first production car, chassis number 7,494 (unregistered for road use at the time of writing), was finished in British Racing Green, with cream interior, chrome wheels and wooden dashboard.

The new engine was designed to minimize the emission of toxic waste and to provide excellent fuel economy, 35 mpg claimed. The engine will also accept unleaded petrol. The combustion chamber in the aluminum head was shaped to produce a swirl effect, which maximizes the amount of fuel actually burned. Ignition was by Lucas with its multi-point hot-wire computerized electronic injection. A large-bore exhaust manifold, which was specially finished in red for Morgan, and aluminumized silencer components comply with the most stringent noise limitation requirements in Europe.

The car will be available with either aluminum or steel bodywork, with galvanized or plastic-coated chassis, and fireproof vinyl or leather upholstery. Other extras available include burr walnut or burr ash dashboard, mohair hood and tonneau cover as well as a choice of 30,000 different twin-pack paint finishes.

The published price for the car on introduction is £13,500 for the two-seater and £14,500 for the four-seater. Extras are detailed in the factory's current price list, which is available for all models.

Prospects

As yet this is an untried and untested model; it is therefore impossible to predict investment potential. At the moment, prototypes and maybe the first ten production cars could increase in value over the years, but it will take time.

Plus 4 Rover-engined

Engine	Rover M16
Type	Four cylinders inline
Bore and stroke	84.5 mm x 89.0 mm
Displacement	1994 cc
Valve	Double overhead cam, belt driven, 4 valves per cylinder
Brake horsepower	138 at 6000 rpm
Chassis	Z section steel pressings, top hat cross-members
Clutch	Single dry plate 242 mm (7½ in.), hydraulic operation
Gearbox	Rover five-speed
Final drive	Open Hardy Spicer propeller shaft to Salisbury hypoid-bevel axle unit
Front suspension	Independent with sliding pillars; coil springs with Armstrong telescopic shock absorbers. Front springs uprated from 4/4 specifications
Rear suspension	Live axle with five leaf springs, and Armstrong lever-arm shock absorbers
Brakes	Girling, hydraulic dual brake system on all four wheels, 9 in. x 1¾ in. rear drums, 11 in. disc front brakes
Wheels	Spoked wire, locking with rotation
Tires	Avon 195/60VRx15, low profile fitted with tubes
Dimensions	Wheelbase 98 in., length 156 in., width 63 in., track 53 in. front, 54 in. rear
Weight	Dry 1,900 lb.

This new twin-cam 16 valve Rover engine at the works waited to be fitted into the latest Plus 4.

Chapter 4

Morgan Plus 8

By late 1965, it was clear that the four-cylinder Triumph TR engines were obsolete. Standard Triumph had to develop a new engine to replace the TR series or die in the sports car market. Its answer was to design and produce a completely new six-cylinder engine for the new Triumph TR5 model. Although there could be no doubt that Standard Triumph would continue to produce the TR4A engine for Morgan for the foreseeable future, obviously it would be only a matter of time before the cost of keeping the factory tooled up to manufacture the small numbers required by Morgan would far outweigh any practical and financial rewards there may have been for the two companies. On the other hand, the physical size of the six-cylinder TR5 engine was such that it was completely impractical to adopt it for use in the Morgan chassis.

Morgan's close association with Ford over the years suggested that the obvious alternative would be to use the Ford V-6 engine. However, the Ford V-6 engine presented just as many problems as the Standard Triumph unit: when offered up in the Morgan chassis, it was both too tall and too heavy. It was obvious that Morgan must continue to produce a high-powered model, capable of continuing the sporting tradition of the company, which had been upheld so well by the Plus 4. The search for an alternative power source continued.

In May 1966, Peter Wilks, a director of Rover Cars Limited called on Peter Morgan at the Malvern factory. Although basically a social call, Wilks intimated during the conversation that Rover would like to enter the sports car market and wondered if Morgan might be receptive to some sort of takeover by Rover. Diplomatic as ever, Peter Morgan replied that he had no intention at that time of selling the company, but if at some time in the future he changed his mind, then he would be pleased to consider Rover's offer.

Another topic of the conversation at the meeting was the new V-8 engine for which Rover had recently acquired the rights to develop and build in the United Kingdom from Buick. Peter Morgan had heard and read a great deal about this engine. It was light and compact and could well be the answer to his problem. However, he also knew that Rover had never been known to supply engines to other motor manufacturers, so he had dismissed the idea from his mind. But at the meeting with Wilks, Peter Morgan tentatively suggested that he would be interested in using the engine in a new Morgan model. To his delighted amazement, Wilks said that there was a distinct possibility that Rover would be willing to supply the Morgan factory with engines.

It so happened that on and off in 1965-66 a motor racing engineer from nearby Upton-on-Severn, named Maurice Owen, who had a serious interest in and liking for the Morgan marque, had periodically approached Peter Morgan asking him if the factory wanted any "special" developments carried out. Each time Peter Morgan had answered no. With production nearly up to maximum, the experienced staff was just not available to take on the development of a new prototype Morgan. However, in light of the Rover offer, Peter Morgan called Owen to the factory to discuss the basic idea with him and decided that he was ideal for the job. Obviously, Maurice Owen was delighted to be invited to join the Morgan company, especially as it coincided with the time that the company he had been working for, the Laystall Racing Team, had just been wound up. Before long Owen was installed in the Research & Development department of the Morgan Motor Company. In keeping with the simplicity in the Morgan factory, this department was a small brick building at the rear of the works—no clinically tiled workshop fitted with the latest electronic equipment for Morgan, just an ordinary concrete floored workshop with a few storage racks, a workbench and so on.

Initial work proved without doubt that using the new V-8 engine was a feasible idea.

Yet full development was hampered by the fact that Morgan only had a non-working mock-up of the Rover engine; Rover had not commenced production of the engine. By devious means, the Morgan factory acquired a new Buick engine, and with the help of Rover's engineers, it was modified to bring it as close as possible to resemble physical and mechanical specifications of the engine that Rover would produce. It was not until 1967 that Rover actually started production of this engine. The main difference between the Rover version and the Buick V-8 engine was that Rover sand cast the engine block as opposed to die casting; Rover also stiffened the webs of the main bearings. There were of course many other minor alterations but none would have adverse effect on Morgan's findings from its research. All the work at both Rover and Morgan was conducted under the utmost secrecy, with few of the Morgan staff knowing what Maurice Owen was working on.

The prototype Plus 8 had two bulges in the bonnet to allow room for the dashpots of the SU carburetors. This led to a comment by at least one enthusiast that it would be fitted with a brassiere rather than a bonnet strap. Note the wire spoked wheels; only two or three Plus 8s were fitted with this type of wheel. The torque experienced on the wheels necessitated a completely new design. This car is currently in the United States.

Plus 8
October 1968–present
Moss or Rover four-speeds ★★★★
Rover five-speeds ★★★

Many modifications were made to the Morgan chassis working testbed. The chassis size was increased by two inches in both width and length, and later the body size was also increased by the same amount. Another feature, which was a departure from the traditional Morgan construction, was the replacement of the wooden floor with a steel one that ran from the pedal board to the seat mounting points. This had the effect of helping to stiffen the chassis and, of course, met with the new regulations being implemented by the US government. The size of the engine necessitated a new type of steering column. It was decided to use a slightly adapted AC Delco-Saginaur collapsible column, which had the added attraction of conforming to the new American regulations. In fact, although shrouded in the most complicated of American legalese, all the requirements that affected the Morgan sports car were incorporated into the new car during the design stage—for example, rocker switches and padded dashboard—although in a few years the regulations were to be altered once more to the detriment of Morgan.

The Moss gearbox used on the Plus 4 was adapted to fit the engine, as was a rear axle from stock. At the same time, the rear suspension was modified to avoid tramping. Owen also called upon his racing experience to design and build special bucket seats to fit the car; these are now made for Morgan by Restall. Wherever possible, Plus 4 body panels were used, and this led to the prototype having two rather sexy bulges on the top of the bonnet to allow for the fitting of the dashpots on the two SU carburetors.

After a last minute hitch, when a faulty alternator burned out some of the wiring, the considerate electrician from Lucas who was carrying out the work agreed to continue to work on into the evening so that the job could be finished that day.

During the whole of its development, Peter Morgan had not interfered in any way with the work that Owen was doing. It was therefore only appropriate that when the car, chassis number R7000, registration number OUY 200E, first rolled out onto a public road under its own power, just after

The Plus 8's bonnet bulges subsequently proved to be unnecessary. The final appearance was in keeping with the established Morgan image.

The famous works' number MMC 11 graced an early example of the model. *John H. Sheally II*

midnight on the morning of February 17, 1967, the driver was its creator, Maurice Owen. Both he and Peter Morgan, who drove it later in the morning, were delighted with the results. The car's handling and power far exceeded their expectations.

Within days of the car's maiden journey, the prospect of a new Morgan model was almost shattered by the politics and financial takeover bids among the big companies. Rover had stretched itself to the financial limits, first with the takeover of Alvis in 1965 and then with the design, development, tooling up and production of several new models such as the Range Rover, the V-8 2000 engine and the three-liter saloons, plus other experimental projects. At the end of 1966, Rover was approached by Leyland Motors with an offer of a buyout. By March 1967, the takeover was complete, with the inevitable changes in policy throughout the new company. Needless to say, one of the questions raised was the need and advisability of supplying the Rover V-8 engine to Morgan, and this was low on the list of priorities. Thus there was no way in which Peter Morgan would be able to launch his new model at the 1967 motor show, as he had hoped to do. Any attempt to force the issue could prove to be disastrous.

The next and almost immediate development was that Peter Morgan was invited to lunch with Harry Webster, the technical director of Standard-Triumph of Coventry, Standard-Triumph having been part of Leyland Motors since 1961. After lunch, Peter Morgan was given a tour of the Triumph engine factory and was shown the complete range, including the V-8 being developed for the Stag. He was asked if he would be interested in using any of the engines, but he replied that having carried out all the research and development of the Rover unit he wished to continue with it.

Next, Peter Morgan was asked to go and see Sir George Farmer, the financial controller of Leyland Motors, who informed him that before Morgan could use the Rover version of the V-8 it would be necessary for Morgan to obtain permission from General Motors. The Morgan world is a small and compact family of owners in all walks of life. It just so happened that one such Plus 4 owner happened to be on the board of General Motors. Peter Morgan contacted him, and the necessary permission was granted in weeks. Yet even this did not speed up the process of whether or not Rover would supply the engine to Morgan.

Drastic needs require drastic remedies. By October, Peter Morgan could see that the procrastination by Leyland Motors was likely to continue indefinitely unless he could find a way to speed up the process. Accordingly, he invited Harry Webster and George Turnbull of Triumph-Rover (the two companies were by this time working closely together as a result of the reorganization after the takeover) to the factory at Malvern Link and showed off the prototype Plus 8. The ploy worked. Before they left, Webster and Turnbull gave assurances that the original agreement between Rover and Morgan was definitely on and that supplies of the engine would start immediately after the launch of the Rover 3500 in April 1968.

Peter Morgan was delighted and immediately instigated an intensive development program under the direction of Maurice Owen. First, it was necessary to prepare the factory for the manufacture of the new model. Next was to implement four improvements to the car as a result of the information they had gathered from the prototype. First, the tremendous performance required far better stopping power. A more powerful servo-assisted braking system was devised and installed. Second, due to the increased fuel consumption from the larger engine, a larger fuel tank was fitted. Third, cast alloy wheels were designed because the car was far too powerful to be run on spoked wheels, although of course the first prototype did. And fourth, a far more complex electrical system than ever before had to be devised to allow the car to conform to the new American regulations, and included such items as an alternator, twin spotlights, three windscreen wipers and hazard warning lights.

All these items were incorporated into two other experimental cars as well. The

The works' number currently shown on the highly successful works racing Plus 8 driven by Charles Morgan, Peter Morgan's son. *John H. Shealy II*

This modified Plus 8 was used successfully in racing by the Stapleton brothers. The oil cooler was below the radiator and the hardtop was custom-built.

first was chassis number R7001, registration number MMC 11, which was Peter Morgan's personal car and which is now in the Motor Museum at Syon Park near London. The second was chassis number R7002, registration number AB 16 (which is now on Peter Morgan's personal Ferrari) was eventually sold to his son-in-law, Lord Colwyn. The original prototype was Maurice Owen's personal car for many years and was eventually sold into the United States.

The total cost of the development of the most powerful car Morgan had ever produced was amazingly low; it did not exceed £14,000. By the time the factory was fully stocked and prepared to produce the new model, the total cost had risen to about £40,000. This of course was only peanuts compared with the hundreds of thousands of pounds or dollars used by major companies to develop a new model. The car was officially launched in October at the 1968 Earls Court Motor Show.

Prospects

The early examples of the Plus 8, providing they are in good condition, are beginning to increase in value. The Rover four-speed gearbox cars are more desirable than the Moss gearbox cars. However, only the Moss gearbox cars were exported to the United States without having to be converted to propane gas. The Rover five-speed gearbox is a distinct improvement on the other Rover gearbox and makes the car far more flexible in the gears; I rank it three stars.

The Plus 8 is an amazing performance car to drive especially when one becomes confident in handling it—not a car for the faint-hearted.

Plus 8
(Specifications at time of introduction, October 1968)

Engine	Rover
Type	V-8
Bore and stroke	88.90 mm x 71.12 mm
Displacement	3528 cc
Brake horsepower	184 at 5200 rpm
Gearbox	Moss four-speed
Fuel supply	Twin SU HS6 carburetors
Chassis	Z section steel pressings, five boxed or tubular cross-members
Final drive	Open Hardy Spicer propeller shaft to Salisbury limited slip hypoid-bevel axle unit
Front suspension	Independent with sliding pillars, coil springs with double acting Girling telescopic shock absorbers
Rear suspension	Live axle with semi-elliptic springs, and Girling lever-arm shock absorbers
Brakes	Girling servo-assisted with 9 in. rear drums, 11 in. discs
Wheels	Cast magnesium alloy, with five-stud fitting
Tires	Dunlop SP Sport 185 VR-15 high-speed
Dimensions	Wheelbase 98 in., length 147 in., width 58 in., track 49 in. front, 52 in. rear. Changed to current measurements of wheelbase 98 in., length 156 in., width 63 in., track 53 in. front, 54 in. rear
Weight	1,820 lb.

Plus 8 fuel-injected

Engine	Rover
Type	V-8, Vitesse fuel-injection
Bore and stroke	89.0 mm x 71 mm
Displacement	3528 cc
Brake horsepower	190 at 5280 rpm
Gearbox	Rover five-speed
(Other specifications identical to Plus 8)	

Plus 8 US Spec

Engine	3528 cc
Number of cylinders	8
Bore and stroke	89 mm x 71 mm
Type of fuel	Propane/butane
Octane	105 plus
Carburetion	Impco 425
Intake manifold	Offenhauser 4 barrel
Compression ratio	9.25:1
Power	155 DIN SAE at 5250 rpm
Fuel tank capacity	18 gal
Touring range	275-325 mi
Weight (wet)	2,140 lb.
Wheels	Cast aluminum

If you are lucky enough to find an early Plus 8, it will more than likely require restoring. Here are two views of an example of the model, body removed. Note the position of the carburetor dashpots that caused the bulges on the bonnet of the prototype. The forward view shows the Moss gearbox and the eroded floor. *John H. Sheally II*

The interiors of new left-hand- and right-hand-drive examples of the Plus 8 passed through the final checking and delivery bay at the Morgan factory in 1988.

Plus 8 engines and transmissions awaited assembly at the Morgan factory.

Plus 8 chassis on trestles with the engine, rear axle and all the other components laid out in order ready for construction. The chassis on the right had a galvanized finish, now offered as an option by the factory.

When Rover was forced to reduce the compression ratio of its V-8 engines in January 1974, due to the new emission control regulations in Europe, the Morgan factory was not at all happy. The reduction meant that the power output dropped from 166 bhp to 143 bhp, which certainly reduced the Plus 8's performance considerably.

At the same time, the owners of aluminum-bodied Plus 8s (aluminum bodies had been offered as an option for several years) who tried to enter production sports car races were refused entry. The scrutineers claimed that these Plus 8s were not eligible because the bodies were only available at extra cost and therefore did not meet the necessary requirements of the homologation regulations.

The timely introduction of the Sports Lightweight model improved on one problem and removed the other. First, the model was bodied entirely in aluminum except for the scuttle and cowl; the car was therefore considerably lighter. Fourteen-inch diameter wheels were fitted to reduce the overall height and to allow for the use of a larger variety of tires. At the same time, the wings were widened to provide room for the six-inch rims required for the new wheels. The track was therefore increased to fifty-two inches at the front and fifty-three inches at the rear. All this made for lively performance, particularly in acceleration especially as the power output had been increased to 155 bhp. The Plus 8 Sports Lightweight's performance was near to the performance of the original Plus 8s.

Introduced at the motor show in October 1975, the Sports Lightweight was offered at the same price as the normal Plus 8, removing any doubts that a scrutineer may have had about extra costs. Production ended in January 1977, and by this time the model had been produced in sufficient quantity to qualify under the second part of the homologa-

The Plus 8 Sports Lightweight was fitted with a roll bar as standard. This example belongs to enthusiast Peter Askew and is fitted with Revolution one-piece wheels. Although not standard, they were a works' approved alternative.

The bumpers on this car are non-original and are color-coded black to the car. The original bumpers were a curved section and fitted with over-riders. *Peter Askew*

Fourteen-inch diameter wheels were fitted to reduce the height, and the fenders widened to make room for the six-inch rims. The front and rear tracks were therefore increased as well. *Peter Askew*

Throughout the fifteen months of this model's production, Rover had been carrying out extensive modifications to its engines in order to try to reestablish the original power output. This coupled with the use of two specially designed four-branch exhausts and an extra resonator on each (which helped to reduce noise levels) brought the power of the base engine back up to 155 bhp. The Sports Lightweight had served its purpose well, and is now a most desirable Morgan production model.

Prospects

Only nineteen cars were made of this model; three were exported and the remainder were sold on the home market. Production ended January 1977.

The true investment model of the Plus 8 is without doubt the Sports Lightweight. The few examples that do come on to the market are eagerly sought after by enthusiasts and investors alike. This is a car for the true and experienced sports car enthusiast, not for the novice. Several examples of this model are fitted with hard tops; this was not stock.

The fascia of the Sports Lightweight included the normal layout plus a tachometer immediately in front of the driver. Because this car is raced, an oil temperature gauge has been fitted to the right of the dash, and a deadman's switch electrical cutout has been fitted on the far right. *Peter Askew*

tion regulations that cover minimum production numbers. So impressed was Morgan with the aluminum body that the company adopted it as standard for all side and rear panels.

Although at least four Plus 8 four-seater cars exist, only one of them was made at the factory. This was built in 1972 as a joint works' experiment and as a special favor for Eric White of Allon White & Son (Cranfield) Ltd., a Morgan main agent. The other cars were built by their owners, and at least one of them was as a result of a rear-end shunt.

The Plus 8 four-seater was far more than simply a graft of a 4/4 four-seater body onto a Plus 8 chassis. The changes in specifications included a larger fuel tank, larger seats (which are fixed) as well as changes to the rear timbers, the bulkhead and the steering shaft measurements. The Plus 8 was also fitted with twin-servo, twin circuit brakes.

There were three reasons for not putting the Plus 8 four-seater model into production, and the same reasons apply with respect to the other experimental car, the automatic-transmission drophead coupe, which was built in 1971, is still owned by the works and is now used exclusively by Jane Morgan, Peter Morgan's first wife. First, production would have meant adding another model to the range at a time when the factory's main interest was in maximizing production of the existing models in order to help reduce the long waiting lists. Second, the four-seater models have to offer a compromise in handling qualities because of the considerable change in weight distribution whenever a third or fourth passenger is carried, nearly all the weight being carried over the rear wheels. This is not as critical in the 4/4, but the greatly increased power and torque of the Plus 8 make it less desirable to offer a car with this performance potential in a form that allows the balance to be so markedly changed with the passenger load. Third, because of the inevitable limited demand for such a car, sales could not justify the cost involved in putting the car into production.

Prospects

Of these two cars, the drophead coupe would be by far the best investment—should it ever come on the market. The four-seater, although rare, is not nearly as desirable.

The only works-produced Plus 8 four-seater was built as an experiment and was subsequently sold to a Morgan main agent for his own use. The wide-section tires and tow bar contributed to the unfamiliar appearance.

Another unique Morgan is this automatic transmission Plus 8 drophead coupe, which was also built as an experiment. After extensive testing, Morgan decided not to put the car into production because of the potential limited demand and because the extra weight adversely affected performance. This car has since been used by Mrs. Jane Morgan as her personal transport. The registration number is JM53. Here it underwent repairs at the works after being involved in an accident.

Engine and chassis numbers

When dating any model of the Morgan, remember that the Morgan Motor Company's year ran from October to September. This calendar evolved to coincide with the dates of the annual motorcycle shows, as it was here that manufacturers announced their new models for the forthcoming year. It therefore follows that it was quite possible to buy a 1928 model Morgan that was first registered in the last three months of 1927. This also applies to four-wheeler models.

Engine numbers on three-wheelers

While reading the three-wheeler section of this buyer's guide, you will find many references to different types of JAP engines, each of which are prefixed by a list of letters. These letters do have a meaning and enable anyone in the know to identify the type of engine immediately. So to remove the mystery, I list a brief guide to their meanings.

K 87.5 mm bore x 85.0 mm stroke
J 80.0 mm bore x 90.0 mm stroke
L 87.5 mm bore x 95.0 mm stroke
T Twin
R Racing
O Overhead valve
W Water cooled
Z Dry sump
C Sports

Therefore, LTWZ means 1100 cc twin, overhead valve, water cooled, dry sump. In the case of any engine used in a Morgan which includes in the prefix the letter Z, that letter also indicates a front-start engine. It

just so happens that the front-start engine was introduced at the same time as the dry sump. Information is also indicated by what letters are omitted. For example, if W is not included, then the engine is air cooled, and if O is missing, then it is a side-valve engine and if there is no T, then the engine is a single cylinder.

When examining an engine, you will usually find that the engine type is followed by an oblique stroke, then a letter, then another oblique stroke and another letter, for example, LTOWZ/C/D. The first part can be translated as outlined, but the next letter is a dating letter. The JAP year, like Morgan's, was also governed by the motorcycle show, which was held in November each year, so all engine modifications or changes were dated as from then. This means that the date identification letters could be different but still refer to the same year. However, throughout the whole of their production, all engine numbers ran consecutively irrespective of size, so that the date of any engine can be worked out very accurately. The letter coding is deciphered below.

P—1920	P—1940
N—1921	N—1941
E—1922	E—1942
U—1923	U—1943
M—1924	M—1944
A—1925	A—1945
T—1926	T—1946
I—1927	I—1947
C—1928	C—1948

S—1929	S—1949
W—1930	W—1950
H—1931	H—1951
Y—1932	Y—1952
Z—1933	Z—1953
D—1934	D—1954
R—1935	R—1955
V—1936	V—1956
F—1937	F—1957
O—1938	O—1958
G—1939	G—1959

The final letter in the sequence was used to indicate to the factory some variation in the car's design. Unfortunately, the exact meanings of the majority of these letters are unknown. In addition, there are usually several letters immediately after the serial number; the meaning of most of these is again unknown, but many meanings have been worked out by stripping and comparing engines with or without certain sets of letters. What is certain is that these letters were intended as identification codes for the factory when a customer ordered spare parts, for example, a larger or smaller than standard main shaft or bearing.

Chassis numbers on three-wheelers

The location of numbers on Morgan three-wheelers is a complex matter; however they basically follow the patterns detailed below.

Three-wheeler Runabouts are not referred to by chassis numbers but are identified by a car number.

However, note that besides the car number the early cars also had what is apparently a chassis number (examples are known to follow in sequence), but these chassis numbers ceased to be used by the middle of World War One. These "chassis numbers" were stamped on the nose piece of the bevel box where it is joined by the torque tube.

The car number was stamped on the right-hand side of the timing cover of the magneto, as viewed from the front when standing facing the car. This practice continued until late 1927, but just a few are known to exist on 1928 cars. In addition, from 1921 to 1929, a single number was also stamped on the flange of the bevel box where it is bolted to the torque tube. The

number is believed to be a year code, for example, 1921 is denoted by a 1 and in sequence to 1929 by a 9. (Examples are known for 1922 by a 2, 1927 by a 7, 1928 by an 8 and 1929 by a 9, but some cars of the same years do not have such a number recorded on them.)

From 1928 to 1952 (a few are known on 1927 cars), the car number was stamped on a St. Christopher dashboard plaque that was about two inches in diameter. At first, these plaques bore the words "Morgan Runabout" around the top and the words "Use Castrol Oil" at the bottom, with a St. Christopher about one inch in diameter in the center and a segment under this stamped "Car Number" followed by the number.

However, in 1934 and 1935, the wording was changed to "Morgan Three-wheeler" and "Use Castrol, Mobiloil, Shelloil" (examples of both types are known in each year). These badges were either fitted on the left-hand side of the dashboard facing the passenger or on the horizontal wooden member of the bodywork beside and slightly in front of the driver.

From 1929 onwards, a true chassis number appeared on the M, D and F chassis and was stamped on the torque tube flange where it was bolted to the bevel box in the case of the two-speeders and the gearbox in the case of the three-speeders. The number was also duplicated on the St. Christopher medallion.

As with all matters Morgan, consult the appropriate Morgan club to clarify any numbers found on a car you may be interested in. Always remember to supply as many numbers as possible and the location of each one when asking a club for identification.

Chassis numbers on four-wheelers

Chassis numbers are always stamped on the top of one of the chassis cross-members on the off-side. In the case of two-seaters, drophead coupes and Plus 4 Plus fixed-head coupes, the chassis number will be found on the member immediately behind the gearbox. On the four-seaters, the chassis number is on the member immediately behind the front seats. On the flat-radiator models of the 4-4 and the Plus 4, the chassis number can sometimes also be found on the reinforcing strip of the hood hinge about six inches from the front.

Occasionally, chassis numbers were also stamped on certain body panels, for example, by the spare wheels and on the wood frame of the door hinge supports. These numbers are sometimes only lightly stamped on the metal or wood and are difficult to read.

It is a sound policy to make a note of as many numbers as possible in respect to the major components of your car—chassis, engine, gearbox, rear axle and so on—which will be most useful if ever you need to order or identify replacement parts. This is particularly important if you are not the first owner of the car, the components of which may have been changed as a result of wear and tear or even an accident. The more numbers you can quote, the better.

Production figures

4-4
Total produced: 1,000
Total exported: 121

4/4
Total produced: 1,081
Total exported: 256

4/4 Series II
Total produced: 387
Total exported: 225
Total exported to US: 157

4/4 Series II Competition
Total produced: 38
Total exported: 18
Total exported to US: 9

4/4 Series II Standard
With Aquaplane head
Total produced: 7
Total exported to US: 6

4/4 Series III
Total produced: 60
Total exported: 42
Total exported to US: 31

4/4 Series IV
Total produced: 206
Total exported: 76
Total exported to US: 44 .

4/4 Series V
Total produced: 640
Total exported: 442
Total exported to US: 235

4/4
Ford 1600 and 1600 GT engines
Total produced: 3,513
Total exported: 1,540
Total exported to US: 68

4/4
Fiat 1600 engine
Total produced: 92
Total exported: 26
Total exported to US: 9

4/4
Ford CVH 1600 engine
Total produced: 1,345
Total exported: 562
Total exported to US: 21

Plus 4 flat-radiator
Total produced: 658
Total exported: 437
Total exported to US: 183

Plus 4 interim- and cowled-radiator
All engines
Total produced: 3,854
Total exported: 2,806
Total exported to US: 2,206

Plus 4 interim- and cowled-radiator
Vanguard engine
Total produced: 130

Plus 4 cowled-radiator
Triumph TR2 engine
Total produced: 338*
*1 flat-radiator model

Plus 4 cowled-radiator
Triumph TR3 engine
Total produced: 1,795

Plus 4 cowled-radiator
Triumph TR4 engine
Total produced: 1,565

Plus 4
Fiat engine
Total produced: 122
Total exported: 38
Total exported to US: 0

Plus 4 Super Sports
Total produced: 104
Total exported: 82
Total exported to US: 45

Plus 4 Lawrencetune
Non Super Sports
Total produced: 9
Total exported: 6
Total exported to US: 5

Plus 4 Competition
Total produced: 42
Total exported: 25
Total exported to US: 10

Plus 4 Plus
Total produced: 26
Total exported: 17
Total exported to US: 10

Plus 8
Total produced as of May 31, 1988: 2,981
Total exported: 1,588
Total exported to US: 188

Plus 8 Sports Lightweight
Total produced: 19
Total exported: 3
Total exported to US: 1

Morgan clubs

I strongly recommend that any Morgan owner or prospective owner join a Morgan club. The advice, companionship and access to spares and technical information is priceless.

Morgan Owners Club of Australia
John Hurst
31 Dorset Street
Epping NSW 2121 Australia

Morgan Sports Car Club of Austria
Fred B. Meyer
Cranachstr 10
1130 Vienna, Austria

Morgan Owners Group Belgium
Gaetan de Ghellinck
117 rue de 1'Eglise
1150 Stockel, Belgium

Morgan Sports Car Club Belgium
Hedwig Rodijns
F Peltzerstr 69
2500 Lier, Belgium

Morgan Owners Group Toronto
Audrey Beer
RR 3
Bolton Ontario L7E 5R9 Canada

Morgan Club of Denmark
Nils-Erik Norsker
Lovspringsvej 18
DK 2920 Charlottenlund, Denmark

Morgan Sports Car Club Denmark
Henning Thyrre
Sommerlyst 26
8500 Grenaa, Denmark

Morgan Sports Car Club
Barry Iles
Hollands Farm/Coombe Green
Birtsmorton/Malvern
Worcs WR13 6AB England

Morgan Three Wheeler Club Limited
Alan Lazenbury
The Woodlands/Holloway
Droitwich, Worcs WR9 7AH England

Morgan Club de France
Jacqueline Frot
20 Rue Daguerre
75014 Paris, France

Morgan Owners Luxembourg
Georges Leurs
19 rue du Parc
8083 Bertrange
Grand Duchy of Luxembourg

Morgan Sports Car Club Holland
Machiel Kalf
Teunis Slagterstr 5
1551 CE Westzaan, Holland

Morgan Club Italia
Ambrogio C. Macchi
Via V Foppa 6
20144 Milano, Italy

Morgan Sports Car Club Japan
Satoru Araki
23-8 Narashinodai 2-Chome
Funabashi-Shi
Chiba, Japan

Morgan Sports Car Club New Zealand
Lloyd Gleeson
3, Rogan St.
Plymouth, New Zealand

Clube Portugues de Automoveis Antigos
Manuel Ramos
Av das Rosas 152
Francelos
4400 V N Gaia, Portugal

South African Morgan Owners' Group
Terry Allan
Box 32403
Braamfontein 2017 South Africa

Morgan Owners' Group Sweden
Ingvar Fredriksson
Rallaevagen 10
S 762 00 Rimbo, Sweden

Morgan-Club Schweiz
Daniel Zoller
Via al Chioso
CH 6929 Gravesano, Switzerland

Morgan-Club Deutschland
Hans Jurgen Bell
Dorstenerstr 100
4630 Bochum, West Germany

Morgan Three Wheeler Club Limited
United States
Spence Young
6614 East Corrine Dr.
Scottsdale, AZ 85254
or Larry Ayers
1490 San Francisco St. #10
San Francisco, CA 94123

Western New York Morgan Owners' Group
Alan Isselhard
16336 Church St.
RD 1
Holley, NY 14470

Northwest Morgan Owners' Group
Jacque Morrison
19425 SE 322nd
Kent, WA 98042

Morgans on the Gulf Morgan Owners' Gp
Tony Frederick
3024 Jarrard St.
Houston, TX 77005

Morgan Plus Four Club
Evelyn Willburn
11423 Gradwell
Lakewood, CA 90715

Morgan Motor Car Club
William Boyles
PO Box 50392
Dallas, TX 75250

Minnesota Morgan Club
George Fink
2608 W 45th St.
Minneapolis, MN 55410

Morgan Plus Four Club, N. California
Brian Keller
Dennis Glavis
3900 Glen Haven Rd.
Soquel, CA 95073

Morgan Owners' Group Great Lakes
Jervis Webb
Webb Dr.
Farmington Hills, MI 48018

¾ Morgan Group Ltd.
Stu and Barbara Ross
160 Fairview Ave.
Long Valley, NJ 07853

Ohio Morgan Owners
Jerry Boston
6625 Ivana Ct.
Mentor, OH 44060

Morgan Owners of Philadelphia
John Moffat
1833 Woodland Rd.
Abington, PA 19001

MOG South
Wynell Bruce
2721 Acworth Due West Rd.
Kennesaw, GA 30144

Morgan Car Club of Washington DC
Ed Zielinski
616 Gist Ave.
Silver Spring, MD 20910

Morgan Regalia Collectors' Society
Winstone Sharples
1802 Summit Dr.
Haymarket, VA 22069

So long . . .

A list of technical terms used in advertising and their meanings.

If they say this	They mean this
Motor quiet	I'm using 60 weight oil
Needs minor overhaul	Needs new engine
Needs major overhaul	Ready for the junkyard
Uses no oil	Just throws it out
Completely gone over	Had the sparkplugs sandblasted
Body fair	You can't see the dry rot
Body good	Touched things up with a brush
Immaculate condition	Had it washed
Concours condition	Had it waxed
Drive it away	I live at the top of a hill
Drive anywhere	Within 10 miles of home
Can be towed	On a trailer
Bowlegged old dog	Your car
Fine old Classic	His car
Desirable Classic	Nobody likes it but me
Rare Classic	Nobody liked it when new
Has Classic lines	Box on wheels
Stored twenty years	The motor is frozen
Completed Morro Bay	On a trailer
Extensive rechroming done	Had the front bumper buffed
Extra parts	I finally gave up on it
Other interests interfere	My wife won the battle
No time to complete	Can't find the parts anyway
Call anytime	I'll sit here 'til I sell it
Good investment	Can't depreciate any more
Rough	It's too bad to lie about
Sharp	Whitewall tires
Need money	I found a better one
Must sacrifice	Can't give it away
Firm	$500 off for cash
Asking	$2,000 off for cash
Leaving for army	Finance company getting mean
New top	Only two years old
Good top	Only leaks on rainy days
Bad top	Nothing but shreds
Solid as a rock	Everything rusted together

Source: Reproduced by kind permission of the Morgan Plus 4 Club of California